GERMAN
MADE EASY
LEVEL 2

An Intermediate German Workbook
To Build Essential Vocabulary And Grammar With Ease
(German Audio Lessons Included)

Lingo Mastery

ISBN: 978-1-951949-94-5
Copyright © 2025 by Lingo Mastery
ALL RIGHTS RESERVED

No part of this book may be reproduced, stored in a retrieval system, or transmitted in any form or by any means, electronic, mechanical, photocopying, recording, scanning, or otherwise, without the prior written permission of the publisher.

The illustrations in this book were designed using images from Freepik.com.

CONTENTS

Vorwort (Preface) 1

Einleitung (Introduction) 2

Hinweise zur Benutzung dieses Buches (Notes on how to use this book) 4

HOW TO GET THE AUDIO FILES 6

Unit I – Wiederholung der Grundlagen (Revisiting the Basics) 7

   1. Das Alphabet und seine Aussprache (The Alphabet and its Pronunciation) 8

   2. Nomen: Geschlecht und Anzahl (Nouns: Gender and Number) 9

   3. Artikel im Überblick: Bestimmt und Unbestimmt
     (Articles at a Glance: Definite and Indefinite) 10

   4. Adjektive und ihre Deklinationen (Adjectives and their Declensions) 10

   5. Verben und ihre Zeitformen (Verbs and their Tenses) 10

   6. Pronomen und ihre Funktionen (Pronouns and their Functions) 11

   7. Präpositionen: Arten und Anwendungen (Prepositions: Types and Uses) 11

   8. Adverbien in der deutschen Sprache (Adverbs in the German Language) 12

   9. Die vier Fälle im Deutschen (The Four Cases in German) 12

   10. Satzstrukturen und Typen (Sentence Structures and Types) 12

Übungen (Exercises) 14

Unit II – Kulturelle Unterschiede und Feste (Cultural Differences and Celebrations) 19

   Section 1 – Traditionen feiern (Celebrating Traditions) 20

     1. Zeitformen: Verwendung und Konjugation (Tenses: Usage and Conjugation) 22

       1.1 Präsens (Present) 22

       1.2 Präteritum (Preterite) 24

       1.3 Perfekt (Present perfect tense) 26

       1.4 Plusquamperfekt (Past perfect tense) 27

1.5 Futur I (Future tense I) 29

1.6 Futur II (Future tense II) 30

Section 2 – Das Oktoberfest genießen (Enjoying Oktoberfest) 34

2. Satzarten und Satzstruktur (Sentence Types and Sentence Structure) 35

2.1 Hauptsatz (Main Clause) 35

2.2 Nebensatz (Subordinate Clause) 35

2.3 Fragesatz (Question Sentence) 36

2.4 Aufforderungssatz (Imperative Sentence) 36

2.5 Die Verwendung von „während" und „währenddessen"
(Usage of „während" and „währenddessen") 37

2.6 Kontraktionen (Contractions) 38

Section 3 – Deutsche Kultur in der Unterhaltung (German Culture in Entertainment) 41

3.1 Pronomen (Pronouns) 42

3.2 Relativsätze (Relative Clauses) 44

3.3 Die Verwendung von „als" und „wenn" im Vergleich
(Using „als" and „wenn" for comparisons) 45

3.4 Das Passiv (The Passive Voice) 47

Übungen (Exercises) 49

Unit III – Natur und Umwelt (Nature and Environment) 55

Section 1 – Die freie Natur erleben (Embracing the Great Outdoors) 56

1.1 Konjunktionen: „entweder ... oder", „weder ... noch"
(Conjunctions: „entweder ... oder", „weder ... noch") 57

1.2 Reflexive Verben (Reflexive Verbs) 58

**Section 2 – Für den Umweltschutz einstehen
(Championing Environmental Protection)** 62

2.1 Die Verwendung von „sowohl ... als auch" (Using „sowohl... als auch") 64

2.2 Der Infinitiv mit „zu" (Infinitive with „zu") 65

2.3 Die Verwendung von „je ... desto" (Using *je ... desto*) 66

2.4 Diminutive (Diminutives) 66

2.5 Derivation (Derivation) 69

Section 3 – Die deutsche Tierwelt entdecken (Discovering German Wildlife) 74

3.1 Partikeln (Particles) 75

3.2 Die indirekte Rede (Reported Speech) 78

3.3 Konjunktiv (Subjunctive) 79

Übungen (Exercises) 84

Unit IV – Reisen und Abenteuer (Travel and Adventure) 91

Section 1 – Reiseplanung (Travel Planning) 92

1.1 Die Verwendung von „wenn", „falls", „sobald"
(Usage of *wenn*, *falls*, *sobald*) 94

1.2 Der Gebrauch von „lassen" (Using *lassen*) 95

1.3 Getrennt- und Zusammenschreibung (Separation and Compounding) 96

Section 2 – Reiseziele (Travel Destinations) 101

2.1 Die Verwendung von „obwohl" und „trotzdem"
(Usage of *obwohl* and *trotzdem*) 102

2.2 Konditionalsätze (Conditional Sentences) 104

2.3 Die Verwendung von „denn" und „weil" (Using *denn* and *weil*) 106

Section 3 – Unvergessliche Reiseerlebnisse teilen (Sharing Memorable Travel Tales) 110

3.1 Die Uhrzeit (The Time) 111

3.2 Redewendungen und Idiome (Idioms and Phrases) 113

Übungen (Exercises) 117

Unit V – Bildung und Karriere (Education and Career) 122

Section 1 – In der deutschen Arbeitswelt erfolgreich sein
(Thriving in the German Workplace) 123

1.1 Final- und Kausalsätze (Purpose and Cause Clauses) 124

   1.2 Nominalisierung von Verben (Nominalization of Verbs) 125

   1.3 Interjektionen (Interjections) 126

  Section 2 – Fort- und Weiterbildung (Professional Development) 130

   2.1 Die Verwendung von „um ... zu" für Zwecke (Using „um ... zu" for Purposes) 131

   2.2 Der Infinitivsatz (Infinitive Clause) 133

  Section 3 – Das Bildungssystem in Deutschland erkunden
         (Exploring Germany's Education Landscape) 138

   3.1 Zusammengesetzte Nomen (Compound Nouns) 139

   3.2 N-Deklination (N-declension) 141

Übungen (Exercises) 144

Unit VI – Hobbys und Freizeit (Hobbies and Leisure Time) 148

  Section 1 – Sportliche Aktivitäten (Sports Activities) 149

   1.1 Satzglieder und Satzstruktur
       (Sentence Components and Sentence Structure) 149

   1.2 Die Verwendung von „bevor" und „nachdem"
       (Using *„bevor"* and *„nachdem"*) 151

  Section 2 – Musik und Kunst (Music and Art) 154

   2.1 Die direkte Rede (Direct Speech) 154

   2.2 Temporalsätze mit „solange" und „bis"
       (Temporal Clauses with *„solange"* and *„bis"*) 156

Übungen (Exercises) 159

Schlusswort (Conclusion) 161

Lösungsschlüssel (Answer Key) 163

VORWORT
(PREFACE)

„*Sprache ist die Quelle aller Missverständnisse*" (Language is the source of all misunderstandings) is a thought-provoking quote by Antoine de Saint-Exupéry (1900 – 1944), famous French writer and pilot. It may sound pessimistic, but it's a reminder of the complexity and depth inherent in every language. The beauty lies in diving into these depths and emerging with a clearer understanding, turning previously perceived barriers into mere stepping stones.

Having embarked on this journey with *German Made Easy Level 1*, you've already taken a peek behind the door of the German language and caught a glimpse of its rich landscapes, both linguistically and culturally. Now, as you stand on the threshold of deepening your knowledge, *German Made Easy Level 2* invites you to step inside and explore the corridors and chambers that make up the mansion of the German language.

Levels A2-B1 of the CEFR framework, on which this book is based, represent a transition – a move from basic proficiency to more independent use of the language. While this level promises to be more challenging, it also offers the opportunity to explore the soul of German literature, music, and cinema. The stories, dialogues, and texts in this book have been carefully curated to reflect the authentic spirit of German-speaking regions, encompassing their traditions, celebrations and everyday life. This book is therefore not just a continuation, but an elevation.

To complement this, we have increased our focus on grammatical structures, providing clearer frameworks and ample examples. Vocabulary lists are more extensive, exposing you to a wider range of words and phrases central to everyday conversation. Interactive exercises, for both individual and group learners, are designed to stimulate thinking, facilitate discussion and encourage collaborative learning.

As Antoine de Saint-Exupéry also said, „*Man sieht nur mit dem Herzen gut*" (One sees clearly only with the heart). As you progress through *German Made Easy Level 2*, may you learn not only the words and syntax, but also the heart and soul of the German language and its rich cultural background. We are honored to guide you further into the labyrinth of Germanic linguistics, and we trust that this tome will be a beacon in your ongoing journey.

EINLEITUNG
(INTRODUCTION)

The decision to learn a new language is rarely taken lightly. As a cognitive endeavor that requires time, effort and unwavering commitment, it often raises a pertinent question: Why this particular language? Among the myriad of languages spoken worldwide, German emerges as a compelling answer to this question for a variety of reasons that span economic, cultural, academic and interpersonal spheres.

Starting with the global economy, German plays a central role. Germany is not only the most populous country in the European Union, but is also its economic powerhouse. As the world's fourth largest economy in terms of nominal GDP, Germany is a leader in several industries, including automotive, engineering, pharmaceuticals and information technology. Major companies such as Volkswagen, Mercedes-Benz, BMW, Siemens, Bosch and SAP are just a few examples of German industrial giants with an extensive global presence. Learning German provides direct access to such industries, making you a preferred choice for roles that require business interactions with these global players.

From an academic perspective, Germany has historically been recognized as an oasis of knowledge. Renowned thinkers such as Kant, Nietzsche, and Einstein were all German speakers. Today, German universities continue this legacy of excellence. Institutions such as the University of Heidelberg, the Technical University of Munich and the Humboldt University of Berlin are frequently ranked among the world's top universities. Germany also offers many scholarships and a growing number of courses taught in English, making it an attractive destination for international students. However, knowledge of the German language can greatly enhance your academic experience in the country, as it allows for greater immersion in the educational environment.

The cultural richness of the German language is vast and varied. Germany has been a melting pot of art, literature, music, and philosophy for centuries. The literary masterpieces of Goethe, Schiller, Thomas Mann and Kafka; the musical genius of Bach, Beethoven, Wagner, and Händel; the philosophical insights of Heidegger, Schopenhauer, and Hannah Arendt – all these luminaries and their contributions become more accessible and profound when approached in their mother tongue. German cinema, with its rich history and critically acclaimed contemporary works, offers another compelling avenue for cultural exploration and understanding.

Moreover, the German language is not confined to the borders of Germany. It is the most widely spoken language in Europe, with significant native populations in Austria, Switzerland, Luxembourg, and Liechtenstein. There are also vibrant German-speaking communities in parts of Italy, Belgium, and even Namibia in Africa. This wide distribution reinforces the importance of German in diplomacy and international relations.

As a language that is both rich in vocabulary and structured in grammar, German sharpens analytical thinking. The process of learning and understanding the nuances of case, gender, compound words and syntactical structures can sharpen the mind, improve overall cognitive abilities and even enhance proficiency in other languages.

On a personal level, understanding German can lead to enriching travel experiences. The landscapes of the German-speaking world, from the Bavarian Alps to the banks of the Rhine, from the historic streets of Salzburg in Austria to the cosmopolitan bustle of Zurich in Switzerland, all become more immersive and meaningful when navigated with an understanding of the local language.

In essence, learning German means equipping yourself with a tool that offers countless benefits. Whether it's advancing in the global job market, immersing yourself in academic research, enjoying cultural treasures, enhancing cognitive skills, or fostering personal connections and understanding, German serves as a bridge, connecting learners to opportunities and experiences that are as profound as they are diverse. It's not just about understanding words and sentences; it's about tapping into a rich tapestry of history, culture, innovation and thought that has shaped and continues to influence countless facets of our globalized world.

HINWEISE ZUR BENUTZUNG DIESES BUCHES
(NOTES ON HOW TO USE THIS BOOK)

This book is sequential, with each unit building on the knowledge gained in the previous one. Those already familiar with basic German pronunciation and orthography may wish to skip Unit I, although it can serve as a valuable review and fill in any gaps in knowledge.

Unit I focuses primarily on pronunciation and spelling, while laying the foundation for basic grammar and terminology. Like all subsequent units, it includes exercises, and the German example sentences are integrated into the audio content.

From Unit II onwards, each Unit is divided into sections which include a German text and/or dialogue, grammatical insights with illustrative examples, exercises and a concluding vocabulary list for that section. At the end of the book, there is a comprehensive vocabulary list, which includes terms from each unit and additional vocabulary sets.

▷ The heading of each grammar section is marked with an arrow pointing to its relevant exercise. At the end of the book, there is a solution key for all exercises.

🎧 This headphone symbol next to a paragraph or dialogue indicates that audio content is available for the corresponding section.

🎧 This headphone with a pencil next to an exercise means that you will need to refer to the corresponding audio content to complete the exercise.

Throughout the book we have included info-boxes with additional content, tips, and recommendations:

ⓘ GUT ZU WISSEN	☞ TIPP
Facts and explanations about culture and language use in Germany, Austria, and Switzerland.	Useful tips and recommendations for learning German.

Supplementary vocabulary sets...	**Grammar overview tables...**
...are presented in these colors and help you increase the number of things you can say and write as you study each unit. They may appear alongside the grammatical explanations within a section or as part of the vocabulary list at the end of a section. They sometimes contain additional word lists sorted by topic or a set of useful phrases, depending on context.	...are presented in these gray tones and contain concise grammatical overviews, often supplemented with example sentences and expressions.

LIST OF ABBREVIATIONS:

adj.	—	adjective	*adv.*	—	adverb
coll.	—	colloquialism	*conj.*	—	conjunction
etw.	—	*etwas* (something)	*fml.*	—	formal
idiom.	—	idiomatic expression	*infml.*	—	informal
interj.	—	interjection	*jmdn.*	—	*jemanden* (= someone; acc.)
jmdm.	—	*jemandem* (= to someone; dat.)	*lit.*	—	literally
n.	—	noun	*part.*	—	particle
pron.	—	pronoun	*v.*	—	verb
prep.	—	preposition	*refl.*	—	reflexive
rel.	—	relative	*sing.*	—	singular
pl.	—	plural	*subj.*	—	subjunctive
tran.	—	transitive	*intr.*	—	intransitive
compar.	—	comparative	*superl.*	—	superlative
neg.	—	negation	*gen.*	—	genitive
dat.	—	dative	*acc.*	—	accusative
nom.	—	nominative	*poss.*	—	possessive

HOW TO GET THE AUDIO FILES

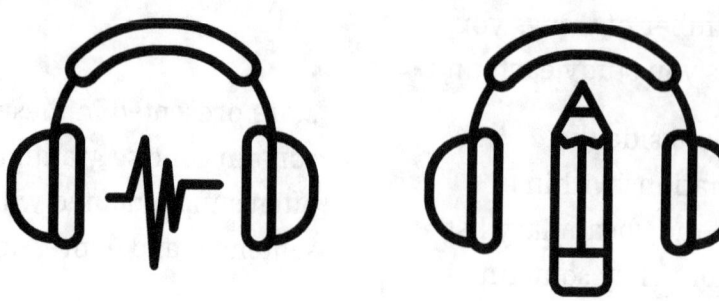

Some of the exercises throughout this book come with accompanying audio files. You can download these audio files if you head over to:
www.lingomastery.com/german-me2-audio

If you're having trouble downloading the audio, contact us at
www.lingomastery.com/contact

Unit 1

WIEDERHOLUNG DER GRUNDLAGEN

(REVISITING THE BASICS)

> Welcome to Unit I – „*Wiederholung der Grundlagen*", a journey back to the essentials of German language. This unit is crafted to refresh your memory and strengthen your foundation in German. We start with the very basics – the alphabet and its pronunciation, ensuring you are well-equipped to pronounce words accurately. As we progress, we will revisit key grammatical components such as nouns, articles, adjectives, and verbs, clarifying their roles and intricacies in sentence formation. By exploring pronouns, prepositions, adverbs, and the four cases, you'll gain a deeper understanding of how these elements interact in German syntax. Finally, we will delve into sentence structures, enabling you to construct clear and grammatically correct sentences. Whether you are revising for proficiency or rekindling your love for the German language, this unit offers a comprehensive refresher course.

1. DAS ALPHABET UND SEINE AUSSPRACHE
(THE ALPHABET AND ITS PRONUNCIATION)

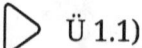 Ü 1.1)

(Find audio on page 6.)

The German alphabet, an extension of the Latin alphabet, is used to script the German language. While it consists of the standard 26 letters found in the English alphabet, the German alphabet also includes several unique characters intrinsic to its language.

Below is a table showcasing the German alphabet, providing pronunciation, the International Phonetic Alphabet (IPA) notation, and an approximate English sound for reference:

LETTER	IPA	APPROXIMATE ENGLISH SOUND	GERMAN EXAMPLE
A, a	[a]	'a' as in "father"	*Apfel* (apple) [ˈapfəl]
B, b	[b]	'b' as in "big"	*Ball* (ball) [bal]
C, c	[ts]	'ts' as in "hits"	*Cäsar* (Caesar) [ˈt͡sɛːzaʁ]
D, d	[d]	'd' as in "dog"	*Dach* (roof) [dax]
E, e	[e]	'a' as in "date"	*Ende* (end) [ˈɛndə]
F, f	[f]	'f' as in "fish"	*Fisch* (fish) [fɪʃ]
G, g	[g]	'g' as in "good"	*Garten* (garden) [ˈgaʁtn̩]
H, h	[h]	'h' as in "house"	*Haus* (house) [haʊ̯s]
I, i	[iː]	'ee' as in "see"	*Insel* (island) [ˈɪnzəl]
J, j	[j]	'y' as in "yes"	*Jacke* (jacket) [ˈjakə]
K, k	[k]	'k' as in "kite"	*Kuchen* (cake) [ˈkuːxən]
L, l	[l]	'l' as in "lamp"	*Lampe* (lamp) [lampə]
M, m	[m]	'm' as in "mouse"	*Maus* (mouse) [maʊ̯s]
N, n	[n]	'n' as in "nose"	*Nase* (nose) [ˈnaːzə]
O, o	[oː]	'o' as in "note"	*Ofen* (oven) [ˈoːfn̩]
P, p	[p]	'p' as in "pen"	*Papier* (paper) [paˈpiːʁ]
Q, q	[kv]	'qu' as in "queen"	*Quelle* (source) [ˈkvɛlə]

R, r	[ʁ]	The German 'r' has no direct English equivalent; it's a guttural sound.	*Rose* (rose) [ʁoːzə]
S, s	[z]	'z' as in "zoo"	*Sonne* (sun) [ˈzɔnə]
T, t	[t]	't' as in "table"	*Tisch* (table) [tɪʃ]
U, u	[uː]	'oo' as in "food"	*Uhr* (clock) [uːʁ]
V, v	[f]	'f' as in "food" or 'v' as in "vivid"	*Vase* (vase) [ˈvaːzə]
W, w	[v]	'v' as in "vase"	*Wald* (forest) [valt]
X, x	[ks]	'ks' as in "box"	*Xylophon* (xylophone) [ˈksyloˌfoːn]
Y, y	[ʏ]	'u' as in "hurry"	*Yacht* (yacht) [jɔxt]
Z, z	[ts]	'ts' as in „wits"	*Zebra* (zebra) [ˈtsɛbʁa]
Ä, ä	[ɛ]	Similar to 'e' in "bed" but more rounded	*Äpfel* (apples) [ˈɛpfəl]
Ö, ö	[ø]	No direct English equivalent; somewhat like 'i' in "bird"	*Öl* (oil) [øːl]
Ü, ü	[y]	No direct English equivalent; somewhat like 'ee' in "see" but with lips rounded	*Über* (over) [ˈyːbɐ]
ß	[s]	's' as in "see"	*Straße* (street) [ˈʃtʁaːsə]

2. NOMEN: GESCHLECHT UND ANZAHL
(NOUNS: GENDER AND NUMBER)

▷ Ü 1.2)

German nouns can be masculine (*maskulin*), feminine (*feminin*), or neuter (*neutral*). Additionally, nouns can be singular or plural.

Gender	Singular	Plural
Masculine	*der Tisch* (the table)	*die Tische* (the tables)
Feminine	*die Lampe* (the lamp)	*die Lampen* (the lamps)
Neuter	*das Buch* (the book)	*die Bücher* (the books)

3. ARTIKEL IM ÜBERBLICK: BESTIMMT UND UNBESTIMMT
   (ARTICLES AT A GLANCE: DEFINITE AND INDEFINITE)

▷ Ü 1.3)

The German language uses both definite and indefinite articles, which are gender-specific.

Gender	Definite Article	Indefinite Article
Masculine	*der*	*ein*
Feminine	*die*	*eine*
Neuter	*das*	*ein*

4. ADJEKTIVE UND IHRE DEKLINATIONEN
   (ADJECTIVES AND THEIR DECLENSIONS)

▷ Ü 1.4)

The declension of adjectives in German depends on the case and gender of the noun they are describing.

Case/Gender	Masculine	Feminine	Neuter
Nominative	*alter Mann* (old man)	*alte Frau* (old woman)	*altes Haus* (old house)
Accusative	*alten Mann*	*alte Frau*	*altes Haus*
Dative	*altem Mann*	*alter Frau*	*altem Haus*
Genitive	*alten Mannes*	*alter Frau*	*alten Hauses*

5. VERBEN UND IHRE ZEITFORMEN
   (VERBS AND THEIR TENSES)

▷ Ü 1.5)

German verbs change according to tense. Here are a few examples with the verb „spielen" (to play):

Tense	Example
Präsens	*ich spiele* (I play)
Präteritum	*ich spielte* (I played)

Perfekt	ich **habe ge**spielt (I have played)
Plusquamperfekt	ich **hatte ge**spielt (I had played)
Futur I	ich **werde** spiel**en** (I will play)
Futur II	ich **werde** ge**spielt haben** (I will have played)

6. PRONOMEN UND IHRE FUNKTIONEN
   (PRONOUNS AND THEIR FUNCTIONS)

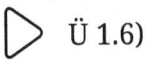

There are various types of pronouns in German, each serving its own purpose.

Type	Example
Personal	*ich* (I), *du* (you)
Possessiv	*mein* (my), *dein* (your)
Relativ	*der, die, das* (who, which)
Interrogativ	*wer?* (who?), *was?* (what?)
Demonstrativ	*dieser* (this), *jene* (that)

7. PRÄPOSITIONEN: ARTEN UND ANWENDUNGEN
   (PREPOSITIONS: TYPES AND USES)

Prepositions can indicate various relationships, including location, time, manner, and cause.

Type	Examples
Lokal	*in, auf, unter* (in, on, under)
Temporal	*vor, nach, während* (before, after, during)
Modal	*mit, ohne* (with, without)
Kausal	*wegen, durch* (because of, through)

8. ADVERBIEN IN DER DEUTSCHEN SPRACHE
(ADVERBS IN THE GERMAN LANGUAGE)

Ü 1.6)

Adverbs modify verbs, adjectives, or other adverbs and can indicate place, time, manner, and cause.

Type	Examples
Lokal	hier, dort (here, there)
Temporal	jetzt, bald (now, soon)
Modal	gerne, schnell (gladly, quickly)
Kausal	deshalb, daher (therefore, hence)

9. DIE VIER FÄLLE IM DEUTSCHEN
(THE FOUR CASES IN GERMAN)

Ü 1.7)

German nouns and pronouns change form based on their function in a sentence.

Case	Function	Example
Nominativ	Subject of the sentence	Der Mann läuft. (The man runs.)
Akkusativ	Direct object	Ich sehe den Mann. (I see the man.)
Dativ	Indirect object	Ich gebe dem Mann ein Buch. (I give the man a book.)
Genitiv	Indicates possession	Das Buch des Mannes. (The man's book.)

10. SATZSTRUKTUREN UND TYPEN
(SENTENCE STRUCTURES AND TYPES)

Ü 1.7)

Different sentence structures serve different functions in German.

Type	Example
Hauptsatz (Main clause)	Ich gehe ins Kino. (I am going to the cinema.)
Nebensatz (Subordinate clause): Relativsatz (Relative clause)	Der Mann, der läuft, ist mein Freund. (The man who is running is my friend.)

Nebensatz (Subordinate clause): Konjunktionalsatz (Conjunctive clause)	Wenn es regnet, bleibe ich zu Hause. (If it rains, I'll stay at home.)
Nebensatz (Subordinate clause): Konditionalsatz (Conditional sentence)	Wenn ich könnte, würde ich reisen. (If I could, I would travel.)

The basic knowledge you've reviewed in this chapter is like the roots of a tree, providing support and nourishment as you branch out into the more complex aspects of the language. Every great journey requires occasional stops to ensure that the path you have already travelled is well understood. With the basics firmly in hand, you will be better equipped to tackle the challenges ahead. Remember Rita Mae Brown's words "Language is the road map of a culture. It tells you where its people come from and where they are going" and think of this journey not just as learning a language, but as discovering a rich tapestry of culture, history and human thought. The road ahead is exciting and full of discovery.

ÜBUNGEN (EXERCISES)

Ü 1.1) Finde für jeden Buchstaben des deutschen Alphabets ein deutsches Wort, das mit diesem Buchstaben beginnt.
Find a German word for each letter of the German alphabet that starts with that letter.

Example: A → _____Arbeit_____

A → _____ B → _____ C → _____
D → _____ E → _____ F → _____
G → _____ H → _____ I → _____
J → _____ K → _____ L → _____
M → _____ N → _____ O → _____
P → _____ Q → _____ R → _____
S → _____ T → _____ U → _____
V → _____ W → _____ X → _____
Y → _____ Z → _____ Ä → _____
Ö → _____ Ü → _____

Ü 1.2) Schau dir die folgenden Bilder genau an. Neben jedem Bild stehen fünf Optionen. Wähle das passende Nomen für jedes Bild.
Look carefully at the following pictures. There are five options next to each picture. Choose the appropriate noun for each picture.

Example:

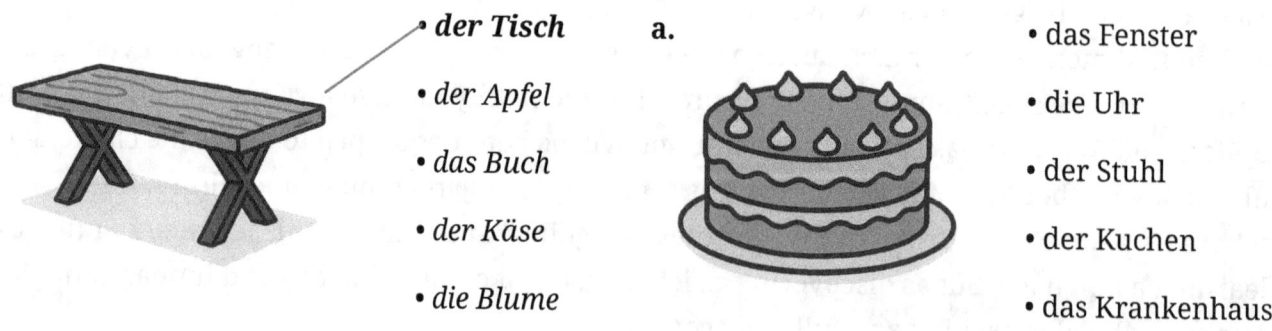

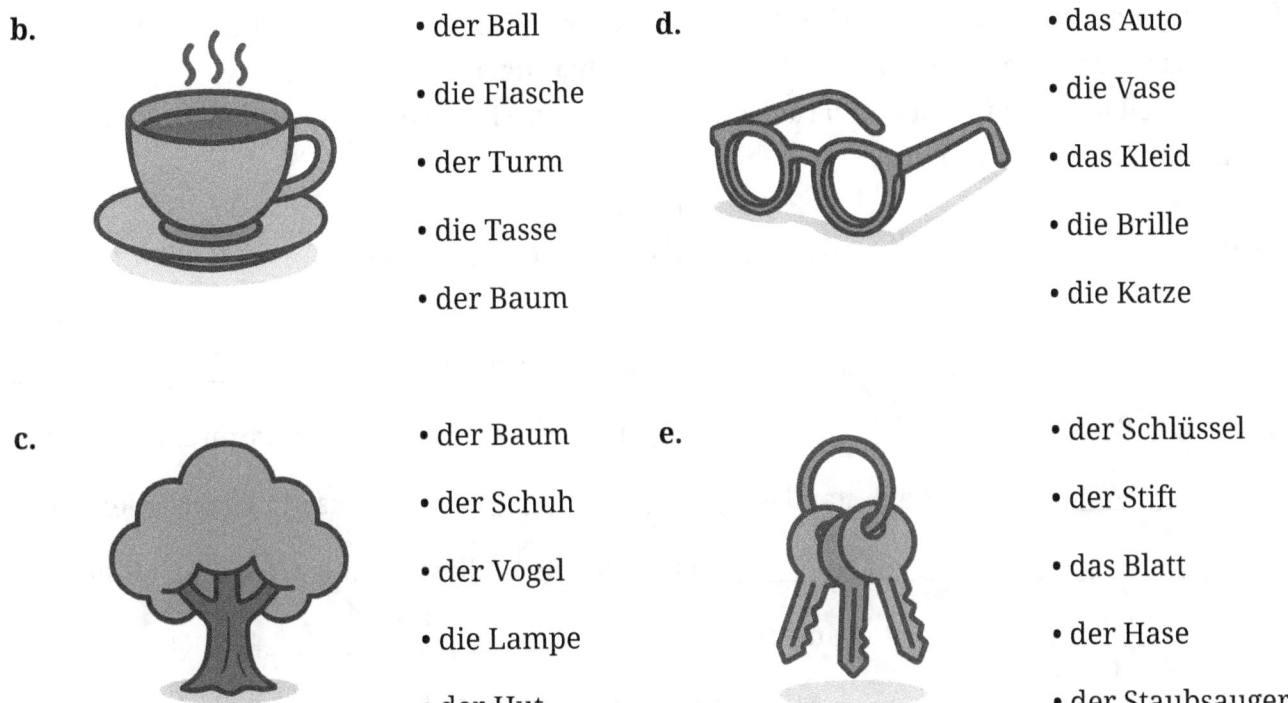

b.
- der Ball
- die Flasche
- der Turm
- die Tasse
- der Baum

d.
- das Auto
- die Vase
- das Kleid
- die Brille
- die Katze

c.
- der Baum
- der Schuh
- der Vogel
- die Lampe
- der Hut

e.
- der Schlüssel
- der Stift
- das Blatt
- der Hase
- der Staubsauger

Ü 1.3) Unten siehst du eine Liste von Nomen und eine separate Liste von Artikeln. Deine Aufgabe ist es, die Nomen mit den richtigen Artikeln zu verbinden. Aber Achtung: Diese Nomen können mehr als einen passenden Artikel haben!

Below you'll find a list of nouns and a separate list of articles. Your task is to match the nouns with the correct articles. But be careful: These nouns can have more than one suitable article!

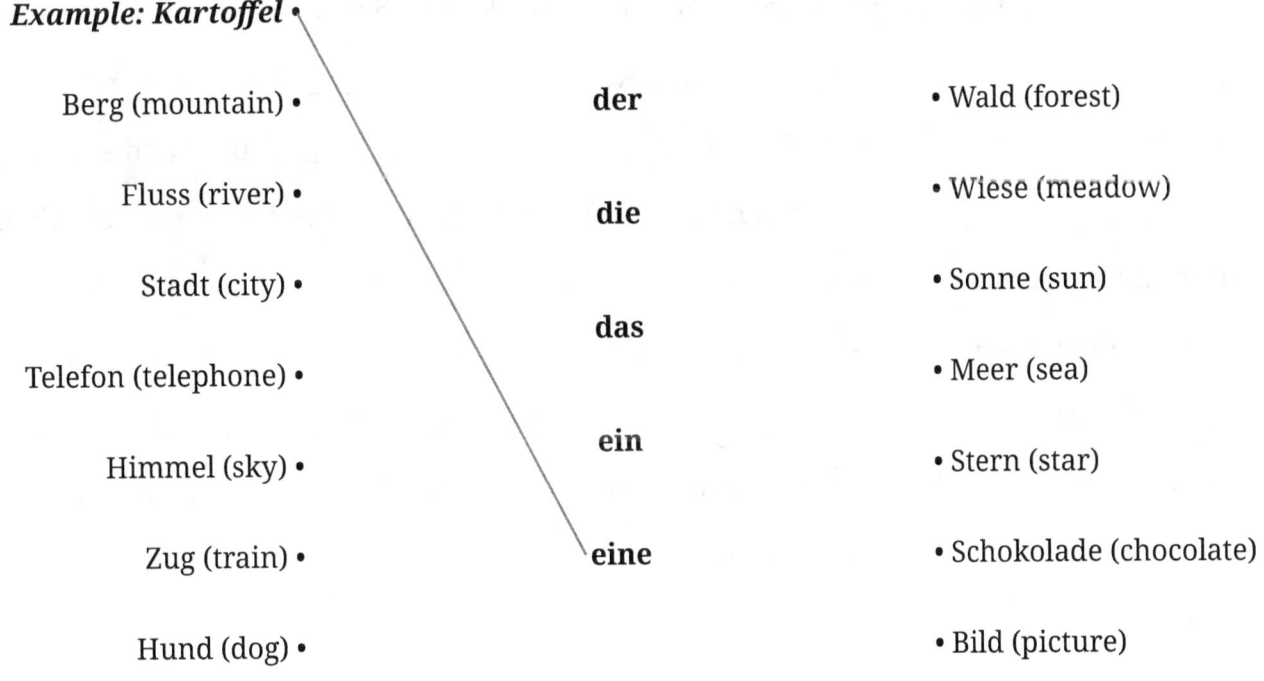

Example: Kartoffel

- Berg (mountain)
- Fluss (river)
- Stadt (city)
- Telefon (telephone)
- Himmel (sky)
- Zug (train)
- Hund (dog)

der

die

das

ein

eine

- Wald (forest)
- Wiese (meadow)
- Sonne (sun)
- Meer (sea)
- Stern (star)
- Schokolade (chocolate)
- Bild (picture)

Ü 1.4) Lies die folgende kurze Geschichte. Es fehlen einige Adjektive. Ergänze die Lücken mit passenden Adjektiven, um die Geschichte lebendiger zu gestalten.

Read the following short story. Some adjectives are missing. Fill in the gaps with suitable adjectives to make the story more vivid.

Example: In der _____**ruhigen**_____ Straße stand ein _____**alter**_____ Verkaufsstand.

Es war ein _____ Tag in Blankenburg, einem _____ Dorf am Fuß eines _____ Berges. Am Rand des Dorfes, direkt neben dem _____ Wald, stand ein _____ Haus mit knarzenden Dielen und _____ Fensterläden. In diesem Haus lebte Frau Müller, eine _____ alte Dame mit einem _____ Lächeln und ihrem _____ Kater namens Gustav. Jeden Morgen, nachdem der Hahn _____ krähte, ging sie in ihren _____ Garten und bewunderte die _____ Blumen, die in der Morgensonne _____ glänzten.

Heute jedoch war etwas anders. Als Frau Müller, wie gewohnt, ihren Kaffee auf der _____ Veranda trank, entdeckte sie ein _____ Paket direkt neben ihrem Lieblingsrosenbusch. Es trug keine Adresse, nur ihren Namen in _____ Lettern. Frau Müller war _____ und entschied, es vorsichtig zu öffnen. Im Paket fand sie einen _____ Brief und ein altes, _____ Foto von ihr als junges Mädchen. Der Brief war von ihrer alten Schulfreundin Klara, die sie seit Jahren nicht mehr gesehen hatte. Klara schrieb, dass sie in die Stadt gezogen war und hoffte, sich bald wieder mit Frau Müller zu treffen. Das Foto war ein Andenken an ihre _____ Jugendtage. Frau Müller war gerührt und beschloss, sofort einen Antwortbrief zu schreiben, in dem sie Klara zu einem Tee in ihrem _____ Garten einlud.

Ü 1.5) Lies den folgenden Text und setze die Verben in den Klammern in die richtige Zeitform.
Read the following text and put the verbs in the brackets into the correct tense.

Example: *Gestern (ich/gehen)* __*ging ich*__ *in den Park.*

Während ich dort (sein) _____, (ich/treffen) _____ meinen alten Freund Peter. Wir (sich/unterhalten) _____ lange und (sich/erinnern) _____ an alte Zeiten. Während unserer Unterhaltung (es/anfangen) _____ plötzlich zu regnen ____. Schnell (wir/suchen) _____ Schutz unter einem großen Baum. Als der Regen (aufhören) _____, (wir/weitergehen) _____ und (sich/verabschieden) _____. Es (sein) _____ ein unerwartetes, aber schönes Treffen.

Ü 1.6) Ergänze den folgenden Text mit den richtigen Pronomen, Präpositionen und Adverbien aus der Box. Nicht alle Wörter werden benötigt.
Complete the following using the correct pronouns, prepositions and adverbs from the box. Not all the words are needed.

Example: *Anna hat ein neues Buch gekauft aber sie hat keine Zeit,* __*deshalb*__ *liest sie es nicht.*

auf	auf	weil	darüber	gegenüber
unter	darin	schnell	hinter	deshalb
darauf	neben	vor	daraufhin	ihnen

Sie legt das Buch _____ den Tisch und geht in die Küche. _____ vergisst sie komplett auf das Buch. Ihr Bruder, der ins Wohnzimmer kommt, bemerkt es und nimmt es in die Hand. Er blättert es _____ durch und findet eine Notiz _____. Neugierig liest er, was auf dieser steht.

Am Abend, als die Familie beim Abendessen sitzt, spricht er Anna _____ an. Anna schaut überrascht, erinnert sich aber dann an das Buch und lacht. Ihr kleiner Bruder sitzt _____ _____ und schaut die beiden neugierig an. _____ möchte er auch wissen, was im Buch steht. Anna verspricht _____, es ihm später vorzulesen.

Nach dem Essen setzt sich die Familie _____ den Fernseher. Doch Anna und ihr kleiner Bruder ziehen sich in ihr Zimmer zurück. _____ dem Sofa kuscheln sie sich zusammen und Anna beginnt, aus dem Buch vorzulesen. Es wird ein gemütlicher Abend, _____ sie ihn gemeinsam verbringen.

Ü 1.7) In den folgenden Sätzen fehlen die richtigen Artikel und Präpositionen. Ergänze die Lücken und bestimme die Satzart.

The following sentences lack the correct articles and prepositions. Fill in the gaps and determine the type of sentence.

Example: Das Buch, das ich für meinen Bruder kaufte, ist sehr interessant. → __**Relativsatz**__

a. Ich gebe _____ Freundin _____ Buch. _____

b. Sie ist die Frau, _____ ich gestern gesprochen habe. _____

c. Er hat einen Hund, _____ sehr groß ist. _____

d. Das ist _____ Haus, in _____ wir wohnen. _____

e. Sie erzählte, _____ sie morgen kommt. _____

f. Der Apfel, _____ Tisch fällt, ist rot. _____

g. Das Mädchen, _____ Bruder krank ist, weint. _____

h. _____ dem Essen gehen wir spazieren. _____

Unit 2

KULTURELLE UNTERSCHIEDE UND FESTE

(CULTURAL DIFFERENCE AND CELEBRATIONS)

Unit II, titled „*Kulturelle Unterschiede und Feste*", offers an in-depth exploration of how the German language intertwines with cultural events and traditions. This unit begins with „*Traditionen feiern*", where you'll learn specific vocabulary and grammatical structures used in discussing German traditions and festivals. As we progress to „*Das Oktoberfest genießen*", the focus shifts to language skills pertinent to understanding and discussing major cultural events like *Oktoberfest*. Here, you'll encounter sentence structures and vocabulary that bring the festivities to life. The unit rounds off with „*Deutsche Kultur in der Unterhaltung*", delving into how German is used in the context of media and entertainment, encompassing pronouns, relative clauses, and other essential aspects of grammar. This unit not only enhances your language skills but also provides a window into the rich cultural fabric of the German-speaking world.

Section 1
TRADITIONEN FEIERN
(CELEBRATING TRADITIONS)

 TRADITIONEN IM VERGLEICH
(COMPARING TRADITIONS)
(Find audio on page 6.)

Young Sara discusses different traditions with her grandfather, Mr. Schmidt, comparing past and present and projecting into the future. They use different tenses to describe their experiences, expectations and the evolution of traditions.

Sara: *Opa, **erzählst** du mir von den Traditionen aus deiner Kindheit?*

Herr Schmidt: *Natürlich, Sara. Wir **gingen** jeden Sonntag in die Kirche, und danach **aßen** wir immer zu Mittag.*

Sara: *Das **ist** interessant. Heutzutage **gehe** ich nur an Feiertagen in die Kirche.*

Herr Schmidt: *Ja, die Zeiten **haben** sich **geändert**. Früher **war** alles anders.*

Sara: ***Glaubst** du, dass wir in der Zukunft wieder traditioneller **werden können**?*

Herr Schmidt: *Es **ist** möglich, dass einige Traditionen wieder **aufleben werden**, aber manche **werden** wohl für immer **verschwunden sein**.*

Sara: ***Hättest** du **gedacht**, dass sich die Traditionen so sehr **ändern würden**?*

Herr Schmidt: *Nein, als ich jung **war**, **konnte** ich mir nicht **vorstellen**, dass so viele Traditionen **verloren gehen würden**.*

Sara: *Wie **findest** du unsere heutigen Traditionen im Vergleich zu denen aus deiner Kindheit?*

Herr Schmidt: *Manche der Bräuche von heute **finde** ich schön, andere **verstehe** ich nicht. Aber so **war** es wahrscheinlich schon immer.*

Sara: *Vielleicht **werden** wir in der Zukunft auch **zurückblicken** und uns **wundern**.*

Herr Schmidt   *Da **hast** du wohl **recht**, Sara.*

DEUTSCHE FEIERTAGE UND BRÄUCHE
(GERMAN HOLIDAYS AND CUSTOMS)
(Find audio on page 6.)

*In Deutschland **feiert** man viele Traditionen und Feiertage. **(Präsens)** So **wurde** zum Beispiel das Oktoberfest das erste Mal im Jahr 1810 **gefeiert**. (Perfekt)*

*Dieses Fest **hatte** seinen Ursprung in der Hochzeit von Kronprinz Ludwig und Prinzessin Therese und **ist** heute eine weltbekannte Veranstaltung, bei der Bier, traditionelle Speisen und Musik **genossen werden**. (Präteritum, Präsens)*

*Viele Menschen **haben** bereits das Vergnügen **gehabt**, an dieser unvergleichlichen Feier teilzunehmen, und die lebendige Atmosphäre sowie die traditionellen bayerischen Leckereien **genossen**. (Perfekt)*

*Ein weiterer wichtiger Feiertag ist der Tag der Deutschen Einheit, der am 3. Oktober **gefeiert wird**, um an die Wiedervereinigung Deutschlands im Jahr 1990 zu **erinnern**. (Präsens)*

*In der Zukunft **werden** vermutlich neue Feiertage und Bräuche **hinzukommen**, die das deutsche Kulturerbe weiter **bereichern werden**. Es **wird** interessant **sein**, zu sehen, welche neuen Traditionen die kommenden Generationen **prägen werden**. (Futur I)*

🛈 GUT ZU WISSEN

Each German-speaking country has its unique ways of celebrating common holidays. For instance, during Easter, in Germany, it's a tradition in some regions to hang colored eggs on outdoor trees, called „Ostereierbäume". In Austria, it's customary to have blessed foods on Holy Saturday, which are then eaten on Easter Sunday. Meanwhile, in Switzerland, there's the „Zwänzgerle" tradition where children challenge adults in a hard-boiled egg tapping contest.

Festtagsbegrüßungen (Festive Greetings)			
German	**English**	**German**	**English**
Frohes Fest!	Happy Holiday!	*Frohes neues Jahr!*	Happy New Year!
Frohe Weihnachten!	Merry Christmas!	*Gesegnetes Fest!*	Blessed holiday!
Ein glückliches neues Jahr!	A Happy New Year!	*Feier schön!*	Have a great celebration!
Herzlichen Glückwunsch zum Geburtstag!	Happy Birthday!	*Zum Wohl!*	Cheers!
Frohe Ostern!	Happy Easter!	*Viel Spaß!*	Have fun!
Alles Gute zum Valentinstag!	Happy Valentine's Day!	*Guten Rutsch!*	Have a good start (into the New Year)!
Herzlichen Glückwunsch zum Jahrestag!	Happy Anniversary!	*Prosit Neujahr!*	Happy New Year! (toast)

1. ZEITFORMEN: VERWENDUNG UND KONJUGATION
(TENSES: USAGE AND CONJUGATION)

▷ Ü 1.1), Ü 1.2)

German tenses help to describe actions in different times. Distinguishing between them is crucial to understanding the nuances of conversation and writing in German. In this chapter we will take a closer look at the different tenses in the German language, their use, conjugation and how they play a central role in German traditions and everyday conversation.

1.1 PRÄSENS (PRESENT)

The *Präsens* (Present Tense) is used to express actions, events, or states that are occurring in the present. In German, this tense is often used to talk about habits, general truths, and also to refer to future events, particularly in conjunction with adverbs of time.

1.1.1 VERWENDUNG (USAGE)

- Describing current actions or states

    Example: *Sara **geht** in die Kirche.*
    (Sara is going to church.)

- Expressing habitual actions

    Example: *Herr Schmidt **geht** jeden Sonntag in die Kirche.*
    (Mr. Schmidt goes to church every Sunday.)

- Referring to general events

    Example: *In Deutschland **feiert** man viele Bräuche und Feiertage.*
    (In Germany, many traditions and holidays are celebrated.)

1.1.2 BILDUNG (FORMATION)

Conjugation in *Präsens* is formed by taking the stem of the infinitive verb and adding the appropriate ending, depending on the subject.

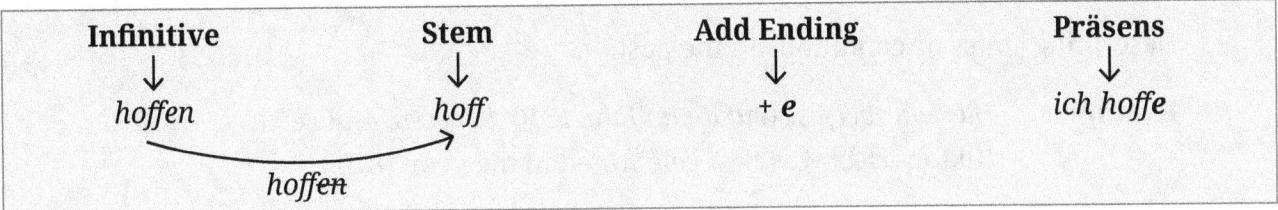

The table below illustrates the conjugation pattern for regular verbs, using the verb „*spielen*" (to play) as an example:

Subject Pronoun	Verb Ending	Example
ich	-e	ich spiele
du	-st	du spielst
er/sie/es	-t	er spielt
wir	-en	wir spielen
ihr	-t	ihr spielt
sie/Sie	-en	sie spielen

1.1.3 BESONDERHEITEN (SPECIAL CASES)

Modal verbs such as „*können*", „*müssen*", and „*wollen*" have irregular conjugations in the *Präsens*.

Example: *Ich kann, du kannst, er kann, wir können, ihr könnt, sie/Sie können*
(I can, you can, he can, we can, you can, she/they can)

Some verbs change their stem vowel in the second and third person singular forms.

Example: „*lesen*" (read) → *du liest, er liest* (you read, he reads)

1.2 PRÄTERITUM (PRETERITE)

The *Präteritum*, also known as the simple past or narrative past, is used to describe actions and conditions that took place in the past. It is most commonly used in written language, especially in narratives, to describe past events, and is less commonly used in spoken German, where the *Perfekt* is preferred.

1.2.1 VERWENDUNG (USAGE)

- Narrating past events or actions.

    Example: *Herr Schmidt **ging** in die Kirche.*
    (Mr. Schmidt went to church.)

- Describing states or conditions in the past.

    Example: *Das Oktoberfest **wurde** im Jahr 1810 das erste Mal gefeiert.*
    (Oktoberfest was first celebrated in the year 1810.)

1.2.2 BILDUNG (FORMATION)

Präteritum conjugations are formed by taking the stem of the infinitive verb and adding the specific *Präteritum* ending. The table below shows the conjugation pattern for regular and irregular verbs, using „*spielen*" and „*sehen*" examples.

Regular verbs		
Subject Pronoun	**Verb Ending**	**Example**
ich	-te	ich spiel**te**
du	-test	du spiel**test**
er/sie/es	-te	er spiel**te**
wir	-ten	wir spiel**ten**
ihr	-tet	ihr spiel**tet**
sie/Sie	-ten	sie spiel**ten**

Irregular verbs	
Subject Pronoun	**Example**
ich	ich s**a**h
du	du s**a**hst
er/sie/es	er s**a**h
wir	wir s**a**hen
ihr	ihr s**a**ht
sie/Sie	sie s**a**hen

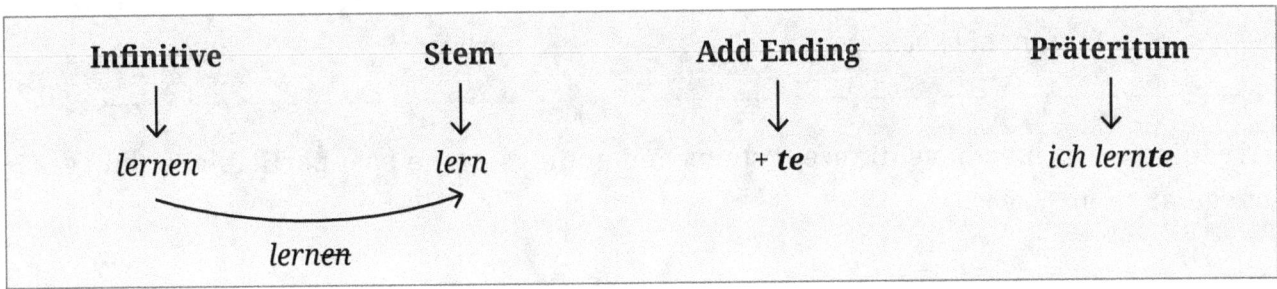

1.3 PERFEKT (PRESENT PERFECT TENSE)

The *Perfekt* is often used in spoken German to discuss past events. It denotes actions that have been completed in the past but are connected to the present, often focusing on the result or the experience of the action.

1.3.1 VERWENDUNG (USAGE)

- Describing completed actions or experiences

    Example: *Herr Schmidt **hat** die Kirche **besucht**.*
    (Mr. Schmidt has visited the church.)

- Talking about changes that happened in the past

    Example: *Sara **ist** älter **geworden**.*
    (Sara has gotten older.)

☞ TIPP

The choice between „*sein*" and „*haben*" as the auxiliary verb can be tricky. As a general rule, „*sein*" is used for verbs indicating movement or a change of state, while „*haben*" is used for other verbs. However, there are exceptions, so it's important to learn them individually.

1.3.2 BILDUNG (FORMATION)

The *Perfekt* is formed using the present tense of the auxiliary verbs „*haben*" or „*sein*" and the past participle of the main verb.

Present of *haben/sein* + ge- + verb stem + -(e)t/en

Irregular verbs may have different stems and endings in the past participle, often „*ge-*" + irregular stem + „*-en*".

Conjugation with „haben"			
Subject Pronoun	Auxiliary Verb	Main Verb (Example: *machen*)	Example
ich	habe	gemacht	ich habe gemacht
du	hast	gemacht	du hast gemacht
er/sie/es	hat	gemacht	er hat gemacht
wir	haben	gemacht	wir haben gemacht
ihr	habt	gemacht	ihr habt gemacht
sie/Sie	haben	gemacht	sie haben gemacht

Conjugation with „sein"			
Subject Pronoun	Auxiliary Verb	Main Verb (Example: *kommen*)	Example
ich	bin	gekommen	ich bin gekommen
du	bist	gekommen	du bist gekommen
er/sie/es	ist	gekommen	er ist gekommen
wir	sind	gekommen	wir sind gekommen
ihr	seid	gekommen	ihr seid gekommen
sie/Sie	sind	gekommen	sie sind gekommen

Perfekt is often used in spoken language, while *Präteritum* is more common in written language, especially in narratives and reports.

1.4 PLUSQUAMPERFEKT (PAST PERFECT TENSE)

The *Plusquamperfekt*, or past perfect tense, is used to describe actions that had been completed before another action in the past occurred. It can also express hypothetical or contrary-to-fact conditions in the past.

1.4.1 VERWENDUNG (USAGE)

- Describing an action that occurred before another action in the past.

    Example: *Herr Schmidt **hatte** das Essen **gekocht**, bevor Sara **kam**.*
    (Mr. Schmidt had cooked the meal before Sara came.)

- Expressing unfulfilled wishes or conditions in the past.

    Example: *Wenn ich das **gewusst hätte**, **wäre** ich **gekommen**.*
    (If I had known that, I would have come.)

☞ TIPP

The *Plusquamperfekt* is equivalent to the pluperfect tense in English, formed with "had" + past participle.

1.4.2 BILDUNG (FORMATION)

The *Plusquamperfekt* is formed using the *Präteritum* (simple past) of the auxiliary verbs „haben" or „sein" and the past participle of the main verb.

Präteritum of *haben/sein*	+	ge-	+	verb stem	+	-(e)t/en

Conjugation with „haben"			
Subject Pronoun	Auxiliary Verb	Main Verb (Example: *machen*)	Example
ich	hatte	gemacht	ich hatte gemacht
du	hattest	gemacht	du hattest gemacht
er/sie/es	hatte	gemacht	er hatte gemacht
wir	hatten	gemacht	wir hatten gemacht
ihr	hattet	gemacht	ihr hattet gemacht
sie/Sie	hatten	gemacht	sie hatten gemacht

Conjugation with „sein"			
Subject Pronoun	**Auxiliary Verb**	**Main Verb (Example: *gehen*)**	**Example**
ich	*war*	*gegangen*	*ich war gegangen*
du	*warst*	*gegangen*	*du warst gegangen*
er/sie/es	*war*	*gegangen*	*er war gegangen*
wir	*waren*	*gegangen*	*wir waren gegangen*
ihr	*wart*	*gegangen*	*ihr wart gegangen*
sie/Sie	*waren*	*gegangen*	*sie waren gegangen*

1.5 FUTUR I (FUTURE TENSE I)

The *Futur I*, or future tense, in German is used to express actions or states that will happen in the future. It often denotes intention, prediction, or assumption regarding future events.

1.5.1 VERWENDUNG (USAGE)

- Expressing actions or events that will occur in the future.

    Example: *Er **wird** gehen.* (He will go.)

- Making predictions about the future.

    Example: *Es **wird** regnen.* (It will rain.)

- Expressing a future fact.

    Example: *In einem Jahr **wird** sie dreißig Jahre alt sein.*
    (In one year, she will be thirty years old.)

- Making polite requests.

    Example: ***Wirst** du mir helfen?*
    (Will you help me?)

> **ⓘ GUT ZU WISSEN**
>
> Although *Futur II* is grammatically correct, it is less commonly used in everyday conversation. Often, context and other tenses are used to convey the same meaning.

1.5.2 BILDUNG (FORMATION)

The *Futur I* is formed using the present tense of the auxiliary verb „werden" and the infinitive of the main verb. The main verb is placed at the end of the clause.

Present of *werden* + Infinitive of the Main Verb

Here's how you conjugate the *Futur I* tense using the auxiliary verb „werden":

Subject Pronoun	Auxiliary Verb	Main Verb (Example: *machen*)	Example
ich	werde	machen	ich werde machen
du	wirst	machen	du wirst machen
er/sie/es	wird	machen	er wird machen
wir	werden	machen	wir werden machen
ihr	werdet	machen	ihr werdet machen
sie/Sie	werden	machen	sie werden machen

1.6 FUTUR II (FUTURE TENSE II)

Futur II, or the future perfect tense in German, is used to express assumptions or speculations about actions that will have been completed in the future, usually before another future event. It's often used to describe future actions from a future perspective.

1.6.1 VERWENDUNG (USAGE)

- Describing actions that will have been completed in the future.

    Example: Wenn du ankommst, **wird** sie schon **gegangen sein**.
    (When you arrive, she will have already left.)

- Making assumptions or speculations about past actions from a future viewpoint.

    Example: Er **wird** es bis morgen **erledigt haben**. (He will have finished it by tomorrow.)

1.6.2 BILDUNG (FORMATION)

The *Futur II* is formed with the future tense of the auxiliary verb „werden", the past participle of the main verb, and the infinitive of the auxiliary verb „haben" or „sein" (depending on the main verb).

Future of *werden* + Past Participle + Infinitive of *haben/sein*

Here's how you conjugate the *Futur II* tense:

Subject Pronoun	Auxiliary Verb (*werden*)	Past Participle (Example: *gemacht*)	Auxiliary Verb (*haben/sein*)
ich	werde	gemacht	haben.
du	wirst	gemacht	haben.
er/sie/es	wird	gemacht	haben.
wir	werden	gemacht	haben.
ihr	werdet	gemacht	haben.
sie/Sie	werden	gemacht	haben.

Traditionen im Vergleich (Comparing Traditions) – *Wortschatz* (Vocabulary)

(die) Tradition (-en) [n.]	tradition
(die) Kirche (-n) [n.]	church
heutzutage [adv.]	nowadays
(die) Zukunft (Zukünfte) [n.]	future
aufleben [v.]	(to) revive
ändern [v.]	(to) change
verschwinden [v.]	(to) disappear
(die) Kindheit (-en) [n.]	childhood
sich (etw.) vorstellen [v.]	(to) imagine
verlieren [v.]	(to) lose
jung [adj.]	young
(der) Vergleich (-e) [n.]	comparison
zurückblicken [v.]	(to) look back
sich wundern [v.]	(to) wonder
recht haben [v.]	(to) to be right
interessant [adj.]	interesting
(der) Feiertag (-e) [n.]	holiday
traditionell [adj.]	traditional
wahrscheinlich [adv.]	probably
immer [part.]	always
(der) Mittag (-e) [n.]	noon

Deutsche Feiertage und Bräuche (German holidays and customs) – Wortschatz (Vocabulary)

feiern [v.]	(to) celebrate
(das) Beispiel (-e) [n.]	example
ursprünglich [adj.]	original
(die) Hochzeit (-en) [n.]	wedding
(die) Speise (-n) [n.]	food
(der) Kronprinz (-en) [n.]	crown prince (male)
(die) Prinzessin (-nen) [n.]	princess (female)
(das) Vergnügen (-) [n.]	pleasure
unvergleichlich [adj.]	incomparable
(die) Feier (-n) [n.]	celebration
lebendig [adj.]	lively
(die) Atmosphäre (-n) [n.]	atmosphere
(die) Leckerei (-en) [n.]	treat
genießen [v.]	(to) enjoy
bayerisch [adj.]	Bavarian
(die) Wiedervereinigung (-en) [n.]	reunion
vermutlich [adv.]	probably
(der) Brauch (Bräuche) [n.]	custom
(die) Generation (-en) [n.]	generation
kommend [adj.]	coming
prägen [v.]	(to) shape

\textit{Musikalische Begriffe} (Musical Terms related to Celebrations)			
German	**English**	**German**	**English**
(das) Lied	song	*(die) Strophe*	verse (in a song)
(die) Musik	music	*(der) Steg*	bridge (in a song)
(der) Tanz	dance	*(der) Puls der Musik*	beat
(die) Melodie	melody	*(die) Pause*	rest (in music)
(der) Rhythmus	rhythm	*(das) Tempo*	tempo
(die) Harmonie	harmony	*(die) Dynamik*	dynamics
(der) Akkord	chord	*(das) Arrangement*	arrangement
(die) Note	note	*(die) Komposition*	composition
(die) Musikgruppe	band	*(das) Musikstück*	piece of music
(der) Sänger / (die) Sängerin	singer	*spielen [v.]*	to play
(der) Chor	choir	*singen [v.]*	to sing
(das) Konzert	concert	*tanzen [v.]*	to dance
(die) Oper	opera	*komponieren [v.]*	to compose
(das) Festival	festival	*dirigieren [v.]*	to conduct
(die) Hymne	anthem	*applaudieren [v.]*	to applaud
(der) Marsch	march	*aufführen [v.]*	to perform

Section 2
DAS OKTOBERFEST GENIESSEN
(ENJOYING OKTOBERFEST)

 GESCHICHTEN VOM OKTOBERFEST
(STORIES FROM OKTOBERFEST)

Anna and Ben discuss the differences and similarities between German and American traditions, using various sentence types and grammatical structures, exploring the correct use of „während", and incorporating contractions.

Anna: *Ben, **findest** du **nicht** auch, dass deutsche Traditionen sich oft sehr von amerikanischen Traditionen **unterscheiden**?* **(Hauptsatz, Fragesatz)**

Ben: *Das **stimmt**, Anna. **Während** wir Amerikaner Thanksgiving **feiern**, **zünden** die Deutschen Kerzen für den Totensonntag **an**.* **(Nebensatz)**

Anna: *Ja, und **während** wir das Essen für Weihnachten **vorbereiten**, **stellen** die Amerikaner ihre Weihnachtsdekorationen schon im November **auf**!* **(Hauptsatz)**

Ben: **Geh'n** *wir tiefer in diese Thematik ein! Was **denkst** du über das Essen? **Meinst** du, es gibt große Unterschiede?* **(Hauptsatz, Kontraktion, Fragesatz)**

Anna: *Absolut! **Nimm** zum Beispiel das Brot. **Während** das deutsche Brot oft dunkel und fest **ist**, **ist** das amerikanische meist weiß und weich.* **(Aufforderungssatz, Nebensatz)**

Ben: *Und **während** die Deutschen ihre Brezeln **lieben**, **bevorzugen** die Amerikaner eher Donuts!* **(Hauptsatz)**

Anna: *So **ist** es! Und lass uns **nicht** die Süßigkeiten vergessen. **Während** die Kinder in Deutschland zu Sankt Martin singen und Süßigkeiten **bekommen**, **gehen** die amerikanischen Kinder zu Halloween von Haus zu Haus.* **(Aufforderungssatz, Nebensatz)**

Ben: ***Sag**, wie **feiern** die Deutschen denn Silvester?* **(Fragesatz, Hauptsatz)**

Anna: *Sie **feiern** mit Feuerwerken und Böllern, **während** viele Amerikaner das neue Jahr mit der Familie oder bei öffentlichen Veranstaltungen **begrüßen**.* **(Hauptsatz, Nebensatz)**

Ben: *Interessant! So **lern'** ich ganz schön viel über die Kulturunterschiede **während** meines Aufenthalts hier!* **(Kontraktion, Hauptsatz)**

> **ⓘ GUT ZU WISSEN**
>
> Starting as a royal wedding celebration, Oktoberfest has grown into a multi-week festival that attracts over six million visitors each year. While Munich hosts the main event, almost every small village and town in Bavaria has its own version of the celebration. With these local Oktoberfest events the scale may vary, the spirit, however, remains the same.

2. SATZARTEN UND SATZSTRUKTUR
(SENTENCE TYPES AND SENTENCE STRUCTURE)

▷ Ü 2.1)

Understanding German sentence structure is essential for effective language learning. German sentences are structured around main and subordinate clauses and can be divided into different types according to their function, such as question sentences and imperative sentences.

2.1 HAUPTSATZ (MAIN CLAUSE)

The main clause can stand alone as it contains all the essential components of a sentence: subject, verb, and object (when applicable).

Structure
Subject + Verb + [Time] + [Manner] + [Place] + [Object]

Example from Dialogue:

„Ben, findest du nicht auch, dass deutsche Traditionen sich oft sehr von amerikanischen Traditionen unterscheiden?"
(Ben, don't you also think that German traditions are often very different from American traditions?)

2.2 NEBENSATZ (SUBORDINATE CLAUSE)

Subordinate clauses cannot stand alone; they depend on the main clause and usually provide additional information.

Structure
[Conjunction] + [Subject] + [Object] + [Time] + [Manner] + [Place] + Verb

Example from Dialogue:

„Während wir Amerikaner Thanksgiving feiern, zünden die Deutschen Kerzen für den Totensonntag an." (While we Americans celebrate Thanksgiving, the Germans light candles for Totensonntag.)

2.3 FRAGESATZ (QUESTION SENTENCE)

These sentences are used to ask questions and are characterized by the inversion of subject and verb or by the usage of question words.

Structure
[Question Word] + Verb + Subject + [Object] + [Time] + [Manner] + [Place]

Example from Dialogue:

„Meinst du, es gibt große Unterschiede?" (Do you think there are big differences?)

2.4 AUFFORDERUNGSSATZ (IMPERATIVE SENTENCE)

Imperative sentences are used to give orders, make requests, or offer invitations. The verb is always in the first position, and the subject is usually omitted.

Structure
Verb + [Object] + [Time] + [Manner] + [Place]

Example: *Sei vorsichtig!* (Be careful!)

Sentence Structures Overview			
Sentence Type	German Example	English Equivalent	Structure (Simplified)
Main Clause	Ben, findest du nicht auch ...?	Ben, don't you also think...?	Subject + Verb + [Other Elements]
Subordinate	... während wir Amerikaner Thanksgiving feiern,...	...while we Americans celebrate Thanksgiving,...	[Conjunction] + Subject + [Other Elements] + Verb
Question	Meinst du, es gibt große Unterschiede?	Do you think there are big differences?	[Question Word] + Verb + Subject + [Other Elements]
Imperative	Lass uns nicht die Süßigkeiten vergessen.	Let's not forget the candies.	Verb + [Other Elements]

„STERB!"

„Der Imperativ von 'sterben' wird mit 'i' gebildet, Du bildungsresistenter Intelligenzallergiker."

„Sterbi?"

2.5 DIE VERWENDUNG VON „WÄHREND" UND „WÄHRENDDESSEN"
(USAGE OF „WÄHREND" AND „WÄHRENDDESSEN")

Understanding the distinction between „während" and „währenddessen" is crucial for describing concurrent events in German, and each word has its own specific usage in a sentence.

„während"	„währenddessen"
„während" is a conjunction used to introduce a subordinate clause, representing the English equivalent of "while" or "whereas". It's utilized to describe something that is happening at the same time as another action, highlighting the contrast between two different events or situations.	„währenddessen" is an adverb meaning "meanwhile" or "in the meantime", indicating that another action is taking place simultaneously with the action mentioned in the main clause. It usually stands at the beginning or in the middle of the main clause, not requiring a subordinate clause for completion.
Structure: Main Clause + *während* + Subordinate Clause	**Structure:** *währenddessen* + Main Clause OR Main Clause + *währenddessen*
Example: *Sie liest ein Buch, **während** er kocht.* (She is reading a book while he is cooking.)	**Example:** *Er bereitet das Essen vor. **Währenddessen** sieht sie fern.* (He is preparing the food, meanwhile, she is watching TV.)
Translation: while / whereas	**Translation:** meanwhile / in the meantime

Knowing when to use „während" and „währenddessen" will help in painting a vivid picture of simultaneous events and emphasizing contrasts or parallels between different actions or states.

2.6 KONTRAKTIONEN (CONTRACTIONS)

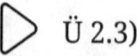 Ü 2.3)

Contractions in German are the result of merging a preposition or particle with an article, which helps to make speaking and writing more fluent and natural. This linguistic phenomenon is particularly common in colloquial speech. Let us focus on contractions that occur in informal speech or dialogue, often reducing the length of words or phrases for brevity and convenience.

Characteristics of *Kontraktionen*:

Often, *Kontraktionen* involve the omission of vowels, and in some cases, consonants are also omitted to form a contraction. Typically observed in informal, spoken German, they might not adhere to the formal, written standards. They are often used in imperative sentences (*Aufforderungssätze*) to give orders, requests or invitations in a more casual way.

Examples from the Dialogue	
Geh'n wir tiefer in diese Thematik ein! **Standard:** Gehen wir tiefer in diese Thematik ein! (Let's delve deeper into this topic!)	So lern' ich ganz schön viel über die Kulturunterschiede während meines Aufenthalts hier! **Standard:** So lerne ich ganz schön viel über die Kulturunterschiede während meines Aufenthalts hier! (This is how I will learn a lot about the cultural differences during my stay here!)

2.6.1 WARUM KONTRAKTIONEN VERWENDEN? (WHY USE CONTRACTIONS?)

- **Efficiency and Brevity:** They make the speech more efficient and brief, especially in informal and conversational contexts.

- **Flow and Naturalness:** They contribute to the natural flow of the spoken language, making interactions more seamless and less formal.

- **Emphasis on Informality:** They emphasize the informal and intimate nature of a conversation, making it suitable for friendly dialogues.

While *Kontraktionen* add to the ease and fluidity in everyday conversations, they are generally avoided in formal writing and professional communications to maintain clarity and formality.

Gebräuchliche deutsche Kontraktionen und ihre englischen Entsprechungen
(Common German Contractions and Their English Equivalents)

German	English
im (in + dem)	in the
am (an + dem)	at the
ans (an + das)	onto the
aufs (auf + das)	onto the
übers (über + das)	over the
ins (in + das)	into the
unterm (unter + dem)	under the
vorm (vor + dem)	in front of the
beim (bei + dem)	at the (with)
zum (zu + dem)	to the
zur (zu + der)	to the (feminine)

Das Oktoberfest genießen (Enjoying Oktoberfest) – Wortschatz (Vocabulary)

sich unterscheiden [v.]	(to) differ
feiern [v.]	(to) celebrate
anzünden [v.]	(to) light
(die) Kerze (-n) [n.]	candle (-n)
(die) Weihnachtsdekoration (-en) [n.]	Christmas decoration
vorbereiten [v.]	(to) prepare
(der) Unterschied (-e) [n.]	difference
(die) Brezel (-n) [n.]	pretzel
bevorzugen [v.]	(to) prefer
(der) Donut (-s) [n.]	donut
(die) Süßigkeit (-en) [n.]	candy
(das) Kind (-er) [n.]	child
(das) Haus (Häuser) [n.]	house
(das) Feuerwerk (-e) [n.]	firework
(der) Böller (-) [n.]	firecracker
öffentlich [adj.]	public
(die) Veranstaltung (-en) [n.]	event
begrüßen [v.]	(to) welcome
(der) Aufenthalt (-e) [n.]	stay
interessant [adj.]	interesting

Praktische Sätze für Kultur & Events
(Practical Phrases for Culture & Events)

German	English
Könnte ich bitte ein Bier/Getränk bestellen?	Could I please order a beer/drink?
Wo finde ich die Toilette im Museum?	Where can I find the bathroom in the museum?
Entschuldigung, wie komme ich zum nächsten Bahnhof?	Excuse me, how do I get to the nearest train station?
Wie viel kostet der Eintritt zum Konzert?	How much is the admission to the concert?
Gibt es eine Garderobe?	Is there a cloakroom?
Könnten Sie mir bitte sagen, wo ich Tickets kaufen kann?	Could you please tell me where I can buy tickets?
Gibt es Ermäßigungen für Studenten?	Are there any discounts for students?
Gibt es einen Audioguide auf Englisch?	Is there an audio guide in English?
Wo ist der beste Ort, um traditionelle deutsche Musik zu hören?	Where is the best place to listen to traditional German music?
Kann ich hier Fotos machen?	Can I take photos here?
Entschuldigung, könnten Sie das bitte wiederholen?	Excuse me, could you please repeat that?
Könnte ich bitte die Speisekarte auf Englisch haben?	Could I please have the menu in English?
Gibt es vegetarische Gerichte?	Are there any vegetarian dishes?

Section 3
DEUTSCHE KULTUR IN DER UNTERHALTUNG
(GERMAN CULTURE IN ENTERTAINMENT)

 MUSIK, KUNST UND KINO IN DEUTSCHLAND
(MUSIC, ART, AND CINEMA IN GERMANY)

*Ein Filmabend mit deutschen Klassikern kann eine faszinierende Reise in die Welt des deutschen Films **sein**. **Diese** sind oftmals Zeugen der Zeitgeschichte und **gewähren** somit einen tiefen Einblick in die deutsche Kultur.*

*Einer dieser Klassiker ist „Metropolis", ein Film, der 1927 **veröffentlicht wurde** und als einer der ersten Science-Fiction-Filme **gilt**. **Es** ist ein Werk, **das** die dystopische Vision der Zukunft **darstellt**, **in der** die Gesellschaft in zwei Klassen unterteilt **ist: die**, die über der Erde **leben**, und **jene**, die unter der Erde **arbeiten**.*

*„Das Boot", **veröffentlicht** in 1981, ist ein weiteres Meisterwerk, **das** die bedrückende und klaustrophobische Atmosphäre eines U-Boots während des Zweiten Weltkriegs **einfängt**. **Dieser** Film **zeigt** das schwierige Leben unter Wasser, während die Crew gleichzeitig mit den Tiefen des Ozeans und dem Feind an der Oberfläche **kämpft**.*

*Wenn man über deutsche Filmklassiker **spricht**, **muss** man auch „Der Himmel über Berlin" erwähnen. Ein Film, der **zeigt**, dass das Leben voller Wunder **ist**, **wenn** man es nur durch die richtigen Augen **sieht**. **Dieser,** 1987 **veröffentlicht**, stellt Engel **dar**, **die** unsichtbar unter den Menschen **leben**.*

*Diese Klassiker **sind** nicht nur Unterhaltung, sondern auch Kunstwerke, **die** ein Stück deutscher Geschichte und Kultur **vermitteln**. Ein Filmabend mit **solchen** Meisterwerken lässt **uns** nicht nur in Nostalgie **schwelgen**, sondern auch die Vielfalt und Tiefe des deutschen Films **schätzen**.*

🛈 GUT ZU WISSEN

Germany is renowned for its classical music heritage, with iconic composers such as Beethoven, Wagner, and Bach. Today, Berlin is a global hub for electronic music and home to the world-famous Berlin Film Festival. Austria, synonymous with Mozart and the Vienna Opera, is also home to the timeless film "The Sound of Music". Switzerland, though more reserved, has made global waves with its Zurich Film Festival.

3.1 PRONOMEN (PRONOUNS)

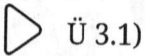 Ü 3.1)

Pronouns in German, like in English, replace nouns to avoid redundancy. They are essential for creating coherent and concise sentences. Pronouns change based on gender (masculine, feminine, neuter) and case (nominative, accusative, dative, genitive). The correct usage of each pronoun is dependent on its function in the sentence and the context in which it is used.

Examples from the dialogue:

„*Diese* sind oftmals Zeugen der Zeitgeschichte und gewähren somit einen tiefen Einblick in die deutsche Kultur."
(These are often testimonies of contemporary history and thus provide a deep insight into German culture.)

"*Dieser* Film zeigt das schwierige Leben unter Wasser, während die Crew gleichzeitig..."
(This film shows how difficult life was...)

	Personal Pronouns			
	Nominative	**Accusative**	**Dative**	**Genitive**
I	ich	mich	mir	meiner
you	du	dich	dir	deiner
he	er	ihn	ihm	seiner
she	sie	sie	ihr	ihrer
it	es	es	ihm	seiner
we	wir	uns	uns	unserer
you	ihr	euch	euch	eurer
they	sie	sie	ihnen	ihrer
You	Sie	Sie	Ihnen	Ihrer

Demonstrative Pronouns	
(Shown in Masculine/Nominative as an example; will change based on gender and case.)	
English	**German**
this	*dieser*
that	*jener*
these	*diese*
those	*jene*

Relative Pronouns	
(Shown in Masculine/Nominative as an example; will change based on gender and case.)	
English	**German**
who/that	*der*
which/that	*welcher*
whose	*dessen*

Possessive Pronouns	
(Shown in Masculine/Nominative as an example; will change based on gender and case.)	
English	**German**
my	*mein*
your	*dein*
his	*sein*
her	*ihr*
its	*sein*
our	*unser*
your	*euer*
their	*ihr*
your (fml.)	*Ihr*

Reflexive Pronouns		
English	**Accusative**	**Dative**
myself	*mich*	*mir*
yourself	*dich*	*dir*
himself	*sich*	*sich*
herself	*sich*	*sich*
itself	*sich*	*sich*
ourselves	*uns*	*uns*
yourselves	*euch*	*euch*
themselves	*sich*	*sich*

Interrogative Pronouns	
English	**German**
who	*wer*
what	*was*
which	*welcher*
whose	*wessen*

3.2 RELATIVSÄTZE (RELATIVE CLAUSES)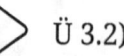

Relativsätze (relative clauses) in German are important tools for constructing coherent, detailed and descriptive sentences. They allow speakers and writers to embed additional information about a noun (antecedent) within a sentence, enriching the narrative without the need for a new sentence. This intricate grammatical structure is an important aspect of German linguistics, reflecting the language's capacity for precision and detail.

To form a relative clause in German, follow these steps:

① **Identify the Antecedent:**

The noun/pronoun in the main clause about which additional information is provided is called the antecedent. In the relative clause, it is replaced by a relative pronoun.

Example: Hauptsatz (Main Clause): *Der Film ist interessant.*
Antecedent: *Der Film*

② **Choose the Correct Relative Pronoun:**

The relative pronoun should match the antecedent in gender (masculine, feminine, neuter), number (singular, plural), and case (nominative, accusative, dative, genitive).

Example: Relativsatz (Relative Clause): *..., der 1927 veröffentlicht wurde.*

③ **Place the Verb at the End:**

In a German relative clause, the conjugated verb is usually placed at the end of the clause.

Example: *..., der 1927 veröffentlicht wurde.*

German Sentence	English Translation
Der Film, **der 1927 veröffentlicht wurde,** gilt als einer der ersten Science-Fiction-Filme.	The movie, **which was released in 1927,** is considered one of the first science fiction movies.

↳ In this sentence, „Der Film" is the antecedent. The relative clause „*der 1927 veröffentlicht wurde*" is providing additional information about „Der Film". The relative pronoun „der" aligns with the antecedent in gender (masculine), number (singular), and case (nominative). Moreover, the verb „wurde" is rightly positioned at the end of the relative clause, conforming to the syntax rules of the German language.

German Sentence	English Translation
„Das Boot", veröffentlicht in 1981, ist ein weiteres Meisterwerk, **das die bedrückende und klaustrophobische Atmosphäre eines U-Boots während des Zweiten Weltkriegs einfängt.**	„Das Boot", released in 1981, is another masterpiece **that captures the oppressive and claustrophobic atmosphere of a submarine during the Second World War.**

↳ This relative clause enriches the main clause by providing supplementary details about „Das Boot", illustrating its ability to depict the atmosphere vividly. It enables a more comprehensive understanding of the film's essence and impact, showcasing the multifunctionality of relative clauses in encapsulating and conveying intricate details and contexts.

Musik, Kunst und Kino in Deutschland (Music, Art, and Cinema in Germany)

German	English	German	English
(die) Musik	music	(die) Skulptur	sculpture
(das) Lied	song	(das) Mosaik	mosaic
(der) Komponist	composer	kreativ	creative
komponieren (Verb)	(to) compose	(die) Fotografie	photography
(das) Konzert	concert	fotografieren	(to) photograph
(die) Musikgruppe	band	ästhetisch	aesthetic
(der) Sänger / (die) Sängerin	singer	(das) Kino	cinema
singen	(to) sing	(der) Film	movie
musikalisch	musical	(die) Schauspielerin / (der) Schauspieler	actress / actor

3.3 DIE VERWENDUNG VON „ALS" UND „WENN" IM VERGLEICH
(USING „ALS" AND „WENN" FOR COMPARISONS)

Ü 3.3)

The German conjunctions „als" and „wenn" play significant roles in creating comparative sentences, allowing speakers to draw contrasts or make comparisons between states, actions, and entities. Though they might appear similar in their comparative functionalities, these conjunctions are deployed in distinct contexts and scenarios within the German language.

The Conjunction „als"	The Conjunction „wenn"
Functionality: „als" is exclusively used for making comparisons between unequal entities or states, and thus, it corresponds to the English "than" in comparative sentences.	**Functionality:** „wenn" is used for comparisons involving equality or similarity, equating to "when" or "whenever" in English, in the context of comparable situations or conditions.
Usage Context: Deployed in comparisons involving the comparative degree of adjectives or adverbs, where a disparity between the compared entities is being conveyed.	**Usage Context:** Employed in hypothetical, conditional, or comparable scenarios where the focus is on equal states or conditions.
Examples: *Er ist größer* **als** *ich.* (He is taller **than** me.)	**Examples:** *Er lacht immer,* **wenn** *er diesen Film sieht.* (He always laughs **when** he sees this movie.)
Application: Utilized when differentiating between disparate quantities, qualities, or states, highlighting a clear divergence between the compared elements.	**Application:** Essential for crafting sentences that portray equal states or scenarios, emphasizing the similarity or equivalence of the conditions being compared.

While „als" brings out differences and inequalities between entities or states, „wenn" is crucial for portraying comparable scenarios or identical conditions. The subtle yet profound difference in their functionalities is crucial in determining the meaning and essence of the sentences in which they are incorporated.

Example for „als":

Das Leben auf dem Land ist ruhiger und entspannter, als es in der Großstadt je sein könnte.
(Life in the countryside is quieter and more relaxed than it could ever be in the big city.)

> ↳ Here, „als" is used as a comparative conjunction to contrast life in the countryside with life in the city, highlighting the greater calmness and relaxation found in rural areas compared to the urban environment.

Example for „wenn":

Ein Film, der zeigt, dass das Leben voller Wunder ist, wenn man es nur durch die richtigen Augen sieht.
(A movie that shows that life is full of wonders when one only looks through the right eyes.)

↳ In this instance, „wenn" is creating a hypothetical scenario, showing the equivalence between seeing through the right eyes and life being full of wonders.

3.4 DAS PASSIV (THE PASSIVE VOICE) ▷ Ü 3.4)

Understanding the passive voice in German is crucial for shifting focus from the doer of an action to the action itself or its receiver. This structure is vital when the doer is unknown, irrelevant, or when the emphasis should be on the action and its effects.

To construct the passive voice in German, a conjugated form of the auxiliary verb „werden" and the past participle of the main verb are used. The past participle is typically positioned at the end of the clause or sentence.

Subject (Nominative) + werden + Past Participle

Active Sentence	Passive Sentence
Der Regisseur **dreht** *den Film.*	*Der Film* **wird gedreht**.
(The director **is shooting** the film.)	(The film **is being shot**.)

In passive constructions, if it's essential to mention the doer of the action, the preposition „von" followed by the doer in the dative case is used. For example, „*Der Film wird* **von dem Regisseur** *gedreht.*" (The film is being shot **by the director**.)

Reflecting on the text provided, the passive voice is evident in sentences like, „*Metropolis, ein Film,* **der 1927 veröffentlicht wurde**," which in English is, "Metropolis, **a film that was released in 1927**." Here, the emphasis is on the action of releasing the film "Metropolis", underlining the importance of the film's release year and not who released it.

To express the time involved in the actions described, different tenses can be formed in the passive voice. Below is a table showing the conjugation of „werden" in different tenses to form the passive voice.

Tense	Example in German	Translation in English
Present	*Der Film wird gedreht.*	The film is being shot.
Simple Past	*Der Film wurde gedreht.*	The film was shot.
Present Perfect	*Der Film ist gedreht worden.*	The film has been shot.
Past Perfect	*Der Film war gedreht worden.*	The film had been shot.
Future I	*Der Film wird gedreht werden.*	The film will be shot.
Future II	*Der Film wird gedreht worden sein.*	The film will have been shot.

Musik, Kunst und Kino in Deutschland (Music, Art, and Cinema in Germany) – *Wortschatz* (Vocabulary)

(der) Filmabend (-e) [n.]	film night
faszinierend [adj.]	fascinating
(die) Reise (-n) [n.]	journey
(der) Einblick (-e) [n.]	insight
(die) Zeitgeschichte (-n) [n.]	contemporary history
oftmals [adv.]	often
(der) Klassiker (-) [n.]	classic
veröffentlichen [v.]	(to) publish
(das) Werk (-e) [n.]	work
dystopisch [adj.]	dystopian
(die) Vision (-en) [n.]	vision
(die) Klasse (-n) [n.]	class
(die) Erde (-n) [n.]	earth
arbeiten [v.]	(to) work
bedrückend [adj.]	depressing
klaustrophobisch [adj.]	claustrophobic
einfangen [v.]	(to) trap / (to) capture
kämpfen [v.]	(to) fight
(der) Feind (-e) [n.]	enemy
(das) Wasser (-) [n.]	water
(der) Himmel (-) [n.]	sky
richtig [adj.]	right
(das) Wunder (-) [n.]	miracle
(die) Unterhaltung (-en) [n.]	entertainment
(die) Vielfalt [n.]	variety
(die) Tiefe (-n) [n.]	depth
schwelgen [v.]	(to) indulge
vermitteln [v.]	(to) impart
lassen [v.]	(to) let

ÜBUNGEN (EXERCISES)

Ü 1.1) Fülle die folgende Tabelle aus, indem du die Verben in den angegebenen Zeitformen konjugierst. Verwende die erste Person Singular.

Complete the following table by conjugating the verbs in the tenses given. Use the first person singular.

Example:

Infinitiv	Präsens	Präteritum	Perfekt	Plusquamperfekt	Futur I	Futur II
lesen	ich lese	ich las	ich habe gelesen	ich hatte gelesen	ich werde lesen	ich werde gelesen haben

Infinitiv	Präsens	Präteritum	Perfekt	Plusquamperfekt	Futur I	Futur II
spielen						
machen						
gehen						
sehen						
schreiben						
kommen						
sprechen						
finden						
bringen						
denken						

Ü 1.2) Du hörst eine Reihe von Sätzen. Deine Aufgabe ist es, das Verb im Satz in der richtigen Zeitform zu konjugieren. Nachdem du die Zeitform konjugiert hast, wird dir die richtige Antwort genannt, damit du dich selbst überprüfen kannst.
You are listening to a series of sentences. Your task is to conjugate the verb in the sentence in the correct tense. After you conjugate the tense, you will be told the correct answer so you can check yourself.

Example: Gesagt wird: „Gehen, Präteritum."
Du sagst: „Ich ging."
Bestätigung: „Richtig! Ich ging."

a. „Schreiben, Perfekt." f. „Kommen, Perfekt."
_____ _____

b. „Sehen, Futur I." g. „Denken, Präteritum."
_____ _____

c. „Machen, Präteritum." h. „Bringen, Futur I."
_____ _____

d. „Spielen, Plusquamperfekt." i. „Sprechen, Plusquamperfekt."
_____ _____

e. „Finden, Futur II." j. „Lesen, Futur II."
_____ _____

Ü 2.1) Bestimme, ob es sich bei den folgenden Sätzen um Hauptsätze, Nebensätze, Fragesätze oder Aufforderungssätze handelt.
Decide whether the following sentences are main clauses, subordinate clauses, interrogative clauses or request clauses.

Example: *Ich bleibe zu Hause, weil es regnet.* → *Hauptsatz* und *Nebensatz.*

a. Ich gehe spazieren, wenn das Wetter gut ist. _____

b. Bringe den Müll raus! _____

c. Wann fährt der nächste Bus? _____

d. Sie liest ein Buch, das auf dem Tisch liegt. _____

e. Wenn du Hilfe brauchst, sage Bescheid. _____

f. Öffne das Fenster! _____

g. Wo ist der nächste Supermarkt? _____

h. Er spielt Fußball, um fit zu bleiben. _____

i. Möchtest du einen Tee? _____

j. Er schreibt einen Brief, der sehr wichtig ist. _____

Ü 2.2) Vervollständige die Lücken in den vorgegebenen Sätzen mit „während" oder „währenddessen". Beachte den Zusammenhang der Sätze und überlege, welches Wort am besten passt.
Complete the gaps in the given sentences with „während" or „währenddessen". Consider the context of the sentences and which word fits best.

Example: Ich lese ein Buch, __während__ mein Bruder schläft.

a. Er kocht das Abendessen, _____ ich das Geschirr spüle.

b. Sie macht Yoga. _____ bereite ich das Frühstück vor.

c. Ich schreibe E-Mails, _____ das Meeting läuft.

d. Er geht joggen, _____ sie die Nachrichten sieht.

e. Ich höre Musik, _____ ich Hausaufgaben mache.

f. Sie malt ein Bild. _____ lese ich ein Buch.

g. Er spielt Fußball, _____ seine Freunde zuschauen.

h. Ich backe Plätzchen, _____ die Kinder spielen.

i. Sie telefoniert, _____ ihr Mann das Auto wäscht.

j. Ich putze das Haus. _____ kauft er Lebensmittel ein.

Ü 2.3) Kontraktionen sind Kombinationen aus Präpositionen und Artikeln, wie „im" für „in dem" oder „zum" für „zu dem". Deine Aufgabe ist es, die Kontraktionen in den folgenden Sätzen zu identifizieren und in ihre ursprünglichen Formen aufzulösen.

Contractions are combinations of prepositions and articles, such as „im" for „in dem" or „zum" for „zu dem". Your task is to identify the contractions in the following sentences and resolve them into their original forms.

Example: Wir treffen uns **am** Bahnhof. ⟶ Wir treffen uns **an dem** Bahnhof.

a. Er geht ins Kino. _____

b. Ich warte beim Arzt. _____

c. Wir lernen fürs Examen. _____

d. Sie sitzt im Café. _____

e. Er ist zum Markt gegangen. _____

f. Sie wollen zur Party. _____

g. Er spielt beim Konzert. _____

h. Wir sind ans Meer gefahren. _____

i. Sie wohnt im Altenheim. _____

j. Ich bin zum Bahnhof gerannt. _____

Ü 3.1) Du hörst einen Text, in dem einige Wörter fehlen. Deine Aufgabe ist es, die fehlenden Pronomen zu ergänzen.

You are going to listen to a text in which a number of words are missing. Your task is to fill in the missing pronouns.

_____ hat mein Buch genommen? _____ lag hier auf _____ Tisch. Ich brauche _____, um meine Hausaufgaben zu machen. _____ _____ und enthält viele interessante Geschichten. Wenn _____ _____ siehst, kannst _____ _____ mir geben? _____ selbst habe überall gesucht, aber _____ kann _____ nirgends finden. Wessen Stift ist _____? _____ sieht fast genauso aus wie _____, aber _____ bin sicher, _____ habe _____ in _____ Tasche getan. Kann derjenige, _____ meinen Stift hat, _____ _____ zurückgeben? Ich brauche _____ für die Schule morgen. _____ ist sehr wichtig für _____, weil _____ _____ Test schreiben werde.

Ü 3.2) Schreibe eine kurze Geschichte oder Beschreibung von etwa 100 Wörtern. In deiner Geschichte sollst du mindestens fünf verschiedene Relativsätze verwenden. Verwende unterschiedliche Relativpronomen und beziehe verschiedene Satzglieder mit ein.
Write a short story or description of about 100 words. In your story, you should use at least five different relative clauses. Use different relative pronouns and include different clauses.

Example: In einem kleinen Dorf lebte einst ein alter Mann, der viele Geschichten kannte. Er hatte einen Hund, der sehr treu war, und ein Haus, das am Rande des Dorfes stand. Das Dorf, in dem er lebte, war bekannt für seine freundlichen Bewohner, die immer bereit waren, sich gegenseitig zu helfen. Der alte Mann saß oft auf einer Bank, von der aus man den gesamten Marktplatz überblicken konnte, und erzählte den Kindern Geschichten, die er in seiner Jugend erlebt hatte.

Ü 3.3) Hier sind einige Sätze mit Lücken, die du ausfüllen sollst. Deine Aufgabe ist es, zu entscheiden, ob in der Lücke „als" oder „wenn" eingesetzt werden sollte, abhängig davon, ob der Satz einen Vergleich oder eine Bedingung ausdrückt.
Here are some sentences with gaps for you to fill in. Your task is to decide whether to use „als" or „wenn" in the gap, depending on whether the sentence expresses a comparison or a condition.

Example: *Er fühlt sich am wohlsten,___wenn___ er in der Natur ist.*

a. Er liest immer, _____ er Zeit hat.

b. Sie war glücklicher, _____ sie jünger war.

c. _____ du das Fenster öffnest, wird es frischer.

d. Ich war gerade eingeschlafen, _____ das Telefon klingelte.

e. Sie geht schwimmen, _____ das Wetter gut ist.

f. Er ist schneller _____ sein Bruder.

g. _____ es regnet, bleiben wir zu Hause.

h. Sie sieht jünger aus, _____ sie ist.

i. _____ er krank war, blieb er im Bett.

j. Es ist schöner, _____ die Sonne scheint.

Ü 3.4) Du erhältst jeweils zwei Sätze. Verbinde sie zu einem sinnvollen Passivsatz. Achte darauf, dass der neue Satz im Passiv steht und inhaltlich richtig ist.

You will get two sentences each. Combine them into a meaningful passive sentence. Make sure that the new sentence is in the passive voice and that its content is correct.

Example: ① *Der Chef prüft den Bericht.*

② *Der Bericht ist wichtig.*

   Der wichtige Bericht wird vom Chef geprüft.

① Der Gärtner gießt die Blumen.

② Die Blumen sind schön.

① Die Lehrerin korrigiert die Klausuren.

② Die Klausuren sind schwierig.

① Der Koch bereitet das Essen vor.

② Das Essen ist köstlich.

① Der Mechaniker repariert das Auto.

② Das Auto ist alt.

① Die Designerin entwirft das Kleid.

② Das Kleid ist elegant.

① Die Kinder bauen die Sandburg.

② Die Sandburg ist groß.

① Der Fotograf macht die Fotos.

② Die Fotos sind scharf.

① Die Studenten lesen die Bücher.

② Die Bücher sind interessant.

① Der Bauer pflanzt die Bäume.

② Die Bäume sind klein.

Unit 3

NATUR UND UMWELT
(NATURE AND ENVIRONMENT)

> Unit III, „*Natur und Umwelt*", is designed to deepen your understanding of the German language through themes related to nature and environmental awareness. The unit commences with „*Die freie Natur erleben*", focusing on language and expressions used in outdoor and nature-related activities. Here, you'll learn how to describe natural scenes, experiences, and actions, using appropriate conjunctions and reflexive verbs. Moving forward, „*Für den Umweltschutz einstehen*" introduces language relevant to environmental advocacy and sustainability, equipping you with the tools to discuss important ecological issues. The unit concludes with „*Die deutsche Tierwelt entdecken*", where the focus is on vocabulary and grammatical structures related to wildlife and nature conservation in Germany. Throughout this unit, you will not only enhance your language proficiency but also gain insight into how environmental topics are discussed in the German-speaking world.

Section 1

DIE FREIE NATUR ERLEBEN
(EMBRACING THE GREAT OUTDOORS)

 EIN SPAZIERGANG IM WALD (A WALK IN THE FOREST)

In this dialogue, Julia and Markus discuss their experiences and preferences while walking in the forest, employing conjunctions, reflexive verbs, reported speech, and the subjunctive mood to convey their thoughts and recount what others have said or might say.

Julia: Markus, ich **freue mich darauf, wieder** im Wald **spazieren zu gehen**.

Markus: Ja, ich auch. Ich **liebe** es, die Vögel zu hören und die Blätter unter meinen Füßen zu spüren. **Entweder** wir **gehen** tief in den Wald hinein, **oder** wir **bleiben** am Rand. Was **meinst** du?

Julia: Hmm, ich **bin weder** ein Fan von dichten Wäldern, **noch mag** ich es, zu weit weg von der Zivilisation zu **sein**.

Markus: Du hast mal **erzählt**, Lisa **habe** dir **gesagt**, tief im Wald **gäbe** es viele interessante Tiere zu sehen.

Julia: Ja, das **stimmt**. Sie **meinte**, sie **habe** sogar ein Reh **gesehen**! Ich **würde sagen**, wir sollten uns **darauf vorbereiten, falls** wir **einigen** Tieren **begegnen**.

Markus: Richtig. Und wir sollten uns auch auf Mücken **vorbereiten**. Ich **erinnere mich**, dass Peter **gesagt hat**, er **sei letztes** Mal von vielen Mücken **gestochen worden**.

Julia: Oh, das **wäre nicht** schön. Wir sollten **also entweder** früh am Morgen **gehen** oder wenn es etwas kühler **ist**. Mücken **mögen weder** Kälte **noch** Wind.

Markus: Ja, **entweder** das ... **oder** wir **nehmen** Mückenspray mit!

🎧 PLAUDEREI UNTER DEN WOLKEN (A CHAT BENEATH THE CLOUDS)

Marie and Tobias find themselves engrossed in a conversation about the weather, using a blend of reflexive verbs, reported speech, and the subjunctive mood to discuss their experiences and what they have heard from others.

Marie: Tobias, ich **freue mich darauf**, endlich **etwas** Sonne zu **sehen**. Es **hat sich** so angefühlt, als **ob** es **ewig** geregnet **hätte**.

Tobias: Ja, wirklich. Ich **kann mich nicht erinnern**, wann es **zuletzt** so viel geregnet **hat**. Es **ist entweder** zu heiß **oder** zu nass **gewesen**!

Marie: Ich **habe gehört**, nächste Woche **soll** es **wärmer werden**. Meine Mutter **hat gesagt**, sie **würde sich wünschen**, dass es ein **bisschen** milder **wäre**.

Tobias: Milder **wäre** wirklich schön. Ich **möchte weder** schwitzen **noch** im Regen **stehen** müssen.

Marie: Das stimmt! Julia **meinte**, sie **würde sich freuen**, wenn wir **entweder** ein Picknick **machen könnten oder** zumindest einen Spaziergang im Park.

Tobias: Oh, ein Picknick **klingt** toll! Und wenn es **regnen sollte, könnten** wir **immer noch** im Café sitzen. Ich **habe gehört**, das neue Café am Eck **habe** leckeren Kaffee.

Marie: Ja, ich **habe auch davon gehört**! Peter **hat erzählt**, er **sei dort gewesen** und der Kaffee **sei** wirklich gut. Ich **hoffe**, wir **können** ihn auch probieren.

1.1 KONJUNKTIONEN: „ENTWEDER ... ODER", „WEDER ... NOCH"
(CONJUNCTIONS: „ENTWEDER ... ODER", „WEDER ... NOCH")

In German, conjunctions play a pivotal role in connecting clauses and coordinating ideas within sentences. „Entweder ... oder" and „weder ... noch" are two conjunctions that express alternate and negative choices, respectively.

„Entweder ... oder" (Either... or)
This conjunction is used to present two alternate options or possibilities, indicating that only one of the options can be chosen.

Structure
entweder + [Option A] oder + [Option B]

↳ **Example:** Entweder wir gehen ins Kino oder wir bleiben zu Hause.
(Either we go to the cinema or we stay at home.)

„Weder ... noch" (Neither... nor)

This conjunction is used to present two negative possibilities, meaning that neither of the options is true or applicable.

Structure
weder + [Negative Option A] noch + [Negative Option B]

↳ **Example:** Ich mag weder Zwiebeln noch Knoblauch.
(I like neither onions nor garlic.)

Usage in Dialogue:

Markus: „Entweder wir gehen tief in den Wald hinein, oder wir bleiben am Rand."
(Either we go deep into the forest, or we stay at the edge.)

Julia: „Ich bin weder ein Fan von dichten Wäldern, noch mag ich es, zu weit weg von der Zivilisation zu sein."
(I am neither a fan of dense forests, nor do I like being too far away from civilization.)

1.2 REFLEXIVE VERBEN (REFLEXIVE VERBS) 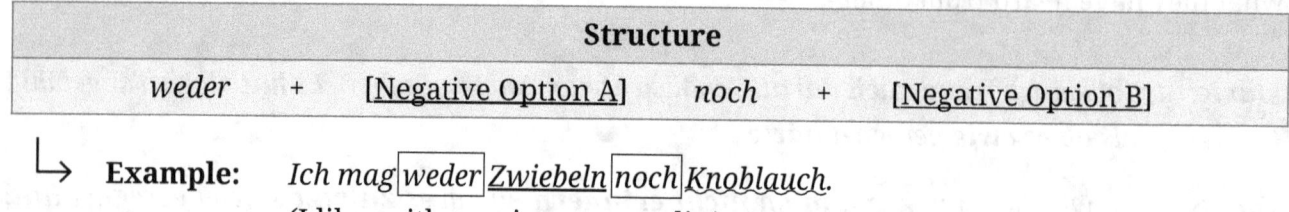 Ü 1.1

Reflexive verbs are essential for expressing actions where the doer and the receiver of the action are the same. These verbs convey a range of actions related to oneself, such as daily routines, feelings and emotions. For example, the verb „anziehen" (to dress) can be used reflexively as in „Ich ziehe mich an" (I get dressed) to indicate that the person performing the action is also the one receiving it. The same verb can also be used non-reflexively as in „Ich ziehe meinen Sohn an" (I dress my son) to indicate that the action is directed toward someone else rather than the speaker.

In German, reflexive verbs use reflexive pronouns to indicate that the action is directed back to the subject. These pronouns are essential parts of the sentence structure and must match the number and case of the subject. In German, for example, the reflexive pronouns are „mich" (myself), „dich" (yourself informal), „sich" (himself, herself, itself), „uns" (ourselves), „euch" (yourselves informal) and „sich" (yourselves formal).

Structure
[Subject] + [Verb] + [Reflexive Pronoun] + [Rest of the Sentence]

Let's illustrate this with examples:

Ich freue mich auf das Wochenende.

(I am looking forward to the weekend.)

Here, „Ich" is the subject, „freue" is the verb, „mich" is the reflexive pronoun, and „auf das Wochenende" is the rest of the sentence, translating to "I am looking forward to the weekend."

Er erinnert sich an diesen Tag.

(He remembers this day.)

In this instance, „Er" is the subject, „erinnert" is the verb, „sich" is the reflexive pronoun, and „an diesen Tag" is the rest of the sentence, translating to "He remembers the day."

In terms of cases, most reflexive verbs use accusative reflexive pronouns, as in „Ich wasche mich" (I wash myself). However, when the sentence has another object in the accusative case, dative reflexive pronouns are used, such as in „Ich putze mir die Zähne" (I brush my teeth).

ⓘ GUT ZU WISSEN

The landscapes of Germany, Austria, and Switzerland offer breathtaking natural wonders. Germany is home to the mystical Black Forest, a vast area of woodland known for its dense trees and folklore. In Austria, the Alps dominate, offering stunning hiking trails, especially in regions such as Tyrol and Carinthia where the Großglockner, Austria's highest peak, marks the border between these two provinces. Switzerland, known for its pristine mountainous regions, is home to the Matterhorn – a pyramid-shaped peak that has become the symbol of the Swiss Alps.

Reflexive Verben: Selbstlernliste mit Beispielen
(Reflexive Verbs: Self-Study List with Examples)

German	English	Example Sentence	English Example
sich vorstellen	(to) introduce oneself	Ich stelle mich dem Lehrer vor.	I introduce myself to the teacher.
sich anziehen	(to) get dressed	Er zieht sich schnell an.	He gets dressed quickly.
sich waschen	(to) wash oneself	Sie wäscht sich die Hände.	She washes her hands.
sich setzen	(to) sit down	Setz dich bitte!	Please, sit down!
sich entspannen	(to) relax	Wir entspannen uns am Strand.	We relax on the beach.
sich konzentrieren	(to) concentrate	Ich konzentriere mich auf meine Arbeit.	I am concentrating on my work.
sich erinnern	(to) remember	Erinnert ihr euch an diesen Tag?	Do you remember this day?
sich beeilen	(to) hurry	Beeil dich, wir sind spät dran!	Hurry up, we are running late!
sich freuen	(to) be delighted/happy	Wir freuen uns über das Geschenk.	We are delighted with the gift.
sich interessieren	(to) be interested	Ich interessiere mich für Kunst.	I am interested in art.
sich ärgern	(to) get annoyed	Er ärgert sich über den Lärm.	He gets annoyed by the noise.
sich langweilen	(to) get bored	Die Kinder langweilen sich ohne Spiele.	The children get bored without games.
sich treffen	(to) meet	Wir treffen uns um sechs Uhr.	We meet at six o'clock.

Ein Spaziergang im Wald (A walk in the forest) – Wortschatz (Vocabulary)

spazieren [v.]	(to) walk
(der) Vogel (Vögel) [n.]	bird
(der) Rand (Ränder) [n.]	edge
(das) Blatt (Blätter) [n.]	leaf
tief [adj.]	deep
dicht [adj.]	dense
weit weg [adj.]	far away
(die) Zivilisation (-en) [n.]	civilization
vorbereiten [v.]	(to) prepare
einige [pron.]	some
falls [conj.]	if
(die) Mücke (-n) [n.]	mosquito
(das) Reh (-e) [n.]	deer
kühl [adj.]	chilly
(die) Kälte (-) [n.]	cold
(das) Mückenspray (-s) [n.]	mosquito spray
(der) Wind (-e) [n.]	wind
mitnehmen [v.]	(to) bring
sich erinnern [v.]	(to) remember

Plauderei unter den Wolken (A Chat Beneath the Clouds) – Wortschatz (Vocabulary)

endlich [adv.]	finally
(die) Sonne (-n) [n.]	sun
sich anfühlen [v.]	(to) feel
regnen [v.]	(to) rain
zuletzt [adv.]	last
nass [adj.]	wet
mild [adj.]	mild
schwitzen [v.]	(to) sweat
(das) Picknick (-e) [n.]	picnic
(der) Spaziergang (Spaziergänge) [n.]	walk
(der) Park (-s) [n.]	park
sitzen [v.]	(to) sit
immer noch	still
lecker [adj.]	delicious
(der) Kaffee (-s) [n.]	coffee
erzählen [v.]	(to) tell
ausprobieren [v.]	(to) try
hoffen [v.]	(to) hope
hören [v.]	(to) hear

Section 2
FÜR DEN UMWELTSCHUTZ EINSTEHEN
(CHAMPIONING ENVIRONMENTAL PROTECTION)

 NACHHALTIGES LEBEN IN DEUTSCHLAND
(SUSTAINABLE LIVING IN GERMANY)

Martin and Franziska discuss different aspects of sustainable living in Germany and illustrate the diversity and flexibility of German grammar through the use of „*sowohl ... als auch*", infinitives with „*zu*", „*je ... desto*", diminutives and derivations.

Franziska: Martin, ich finde, in Deutschland leben wir **sowohl** umweltbewusst **als auch** nachhaltig.

Martin: Das stimmt, Franziska! Viele Menschen hier versuchen **Müll zu reduzieren, zu recyceln** und **zu kompostieren**.

Franziska: Ja, und ich finde, **je** mehr wir uns bemühen, **desto** besser wird unsere Umwelt geschützt. Stimmst du mir zu?

Martin: Absolut! Und viele Städte unterstützen **sowohl** Fahrradfahrer **als auch** die öffentlichen Verkehrsmittel, um den CO_2-Ausstoß zu minimieren.

Franziska: Genau! Hast du die kleinen **Bäumchen** gesehen, die neulich in der Stadt gepflanzt wurden? Sie werden **sowohl** Schatten **als auch** frische Luft spenden.

Martin: Ja, diese **Bäumchen** sind wirklich entzückend! Und ich finde es toll, wie die Leute hier die Bedeutung von Bäumen verstehen. Die Kinder lernen, sie **zu pflanzen** und **zu pflegen**.

Franziska: **Je** mehr wir die Natur schützen, **desto** mehr Wertschätzung entwickeln wir für unsere Umwelt und beginnen, umweltfreundlicher **zu leben**.

Martin: Stimmt! Und ich habe gehört, dass **sowohl** Schulen **als auch** Universitäten Projekte für nachhaltiges Leben anbieten, um das Bewusstsein für dieses **zu schärfen**.

Franziska: Das ist eine tolle Initiative! Denn nicht nur die ältere, sondern auch schon die jüngere Generation, kann viel lernen und dadurch beitragen.

DEUTSCHLANDS BEMÜHUNGEN UM DEN UMWELTSCHUTZ
(GERMANY'S EFFORTS IN ENVIRONMENTAL PROTECTION)

Armin and Julia have a conversation about Germany's various efforts to protect the environment, using different grammatical structures to express different opinions and facts on the subject.

Armin: *Julia, hast du gewusst, dass Deutschland **sowohl** in der Entwicklung von umweltfreundlichen Technologien **als auch** im Naturschutz sehr aktiv **ist**?*

Julia: *Oh ja, in Deutschland **versucht** man, einen großen Beitrag **zu leisten**. Es ist wirklich erstaunlich **zu sehen**, wie viele innovative Lösungen **hier** entwickelt **werden**.*

Armin: *Richtig, **je mehr** wir in erneuerbare Energien **investieren**, **desto besser** können wir unseren Planeten schützen!*

Julia: *Ganz genau! Und ich finde es toll, dass wir **sowohl** Windkraft **als auch** Solarenergie nutzen.*

Armin: *Das **stimmt**. Hast du gehört, dass viele Städte nun **Bäumchen** pflanzen und **Bienenstöcke** aufstellen, um die Vielfalt zu fördern?*

Julia: *Ja, es ist eine wunderbare Initiative! Diese kleinen **Bäumchen** und auch die **Bienenstöcke** können auf lange Sicht einen großen Unterschied machen. Und durch die **Anwendung** neuer, nachhaltiger Methoden können wir den CO2-Ausstoß reduzieren.*

Armin: *Absolut! Es ist wichtig, **sowohl** die Tierwelt **als auch** die Pflanzenwelt **zu schützen**. Die Bemühungen um den Umweltschutz in Deutschland sind wirklich vorbildlich.*

Julia: *Das **sehe** ich auch so. Und **je mehr** wir uns für den Umweltschutz **einsetzen**, **desto lebenswerter** wird unsere Welt für die nächsten Generationen.*

2.1 DIE VERWENDUNG VON „SOWOHL ... ALS AUCH" (USING „SOWOHL... ALS AUCH")

The conjunction „*sowohl ... als auch*" is used in German to express the concept of "both ... and" in English. It is utilized to combine two or more items or concepts, indicating that each item is applicable.

Structure
sowohl + [Statement 1] + als auch + [Statement 2]

The structure „*sowohl ... als auch*" is quite straightforward. It simply connects two elements or clauses, emphasizing that both are included. It's crucial to understand that the entities connected by „*sowohl ... als auch*" are generally of the same grammatical type, i.e., both nouns, both verbs, both adjectives, etc.

	Examples
Connecting Nouns	Deutschland unterstützt **sowohl** erneuerbare Energien **als auch** den Umweltschutz. (Germany supports **both** renewable energy **and** environmental protection.)
Connecting Verbs	Ich mag **sowohl** lesen **als auch** schreiben. (I like **both** reading **and** writing.)
Connecting Clauses	Sie arbeitet **sowohl** schnell **als auch** effizient. (She works **both** quickly **and** efficiently.)

In a main clause, the conjugated <u>verb</u> is typically in the <u>second position</u>.

↳ *Er <u>kann</u> sowohl Klavier als auch Gitarre spielen.*
   (He can play both piano and guitar.)

In a subordinate clause, the conjugated <u>verb</u> usually comes <u>at the end</u> of the clause.

↳ *Ich freue mich, dass er sowohl Klavier als auch Gitarre spielen <u>kann</u>.*
   (I am happy that he can play both piano and guitar.)

When <u>„*sowohl ... als auch*"</u> encompasses entire clauses, it usually comes <u>at the beginning</u> of each clause it is connecting.

↳ *<u>Sowohl</u> die Kinder <u>als auch</u> die Erwachsenen müssen lernen, umweltbewusst zu leben.*
   (Both the children and the adults must learn to live environmentally conscious.)

2.2 DER INFINITIV MIT „ZU" (INFINITIVE WITH „ZU")

▷ Ü 2.1)

The infinitive with „zu" in German is equivalent to the English infinitive form with "to", such as "to do". It is used when an action is described but not assigned to a subject, making it particularly common with verbs of perception, preference, and probability, among others.

Structure
[Conjugated Verb] + zu + [Infinitive Verb]

Note: The infinitive verb is always placed at the end of the clause when using „zu".

„Der Infinitiv mit zu" is generally used after certain verbs, adjectives, and nouns, as well as in constructions expressing an opinion or assumption. The word „zu" is placed before the infinitive verb, connecting it to the rest of the sentence.

Examples	
After Certain Verbs	Ich hoffe, bald wieder **zu reisen**. (I hope to travel again soon.)
After Certain Nouns	Ich habe die Absicht, Deutsch **zu lernen**. (I have the intention to learn German.)
With Constructions	Es ist wichtig, täglich **zu üben**. (It is important to practice daily.)

> The <u>conjugated verb</u>'s position in the sentence is dependent on whether it is in a main or a subordinate clause.
>
> Ich <u>glaube</u>, das Problem zu verstehen.   Ich bin froh, dass ich Zeit <u>habe</u> zu lesen.
> (I believe to understand the problem.)   (I am glad that I have time to read.)

> A <u>comma</u> is often used in subordinate clauses, and sometimes in main clauses if the sentence is complex.
>
> Er ist traurig, nicht eingeladen worden zu sein.   Ich hoffe, nach der Arbeit bald schlafen zu können.
> (He is sad not to have been invited.)   (I hope to sleep soon after work.)

> Not every verb can be used with „der Infinitiv mit zu". Only specific verbs, nouns, and constructions require „zu" before an infinitive verb.
>
> Er verspricht, pünktlich <u>zu kommen</u>.   Er will <u>schlafen</u>.
> (He promises to come on time.)   (He wants to sleep.)

2.3 DIE VERWENDUNG VON „JE ... DESTO"
(USING „JE ... DESTO")

The „je ... desto" construction is used when there's a proportional relationship between two situations. The first part of the sentence begins with „je" and describes a change in quantity or quality, while the second part, beginning with „desto", outlines the consequence of that change.

Structure
je + [comparative adjective/adverb] + , + desto + [comparative adjective/adverb]

Examples	
Expressing Proportionality	*Je länger man in Deutschland lebt, desto besser versteht man die Kultur.* (The longer you live in Germany, the better you understand the culture.)
Reflecting Dependency	*Je mehr ich lerne, desto mehr verstehe ich.* (The more I learn, the more I understand.)
Describing Relationship	*Je älter ich werde, desto mehr weiß ich meine Familie zu schätzen.* (The older I get, the more I appreciate my family.)

2.4 DIMINUTIVE
(DIMINUTIVES)

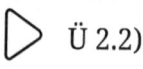 Ü 2.2)

Diminutives are chiefly employed to render a noun more intimate, to shrink its conceptual size, or to reflect its youth or smallness in actuality. The German language accomplishes this through the addition of specific suffixes, primarily *-chen* and *-lein*, to the base noun. Regardless of the original gender of the noun, the noun transformed by the diminutive suffix is always of neuter gender, carrying the article „*das*".

The formation of diminutives is a straightforward process. It involves appending the suffix *-chen* or *-lein* to the base noun. However, the application of these suffixes is not wholly interchangeable, as the usage of *-chen* is far more prevalent, and *-lein* is more habitually utilized in the southern regions of Germany.

Structure
Base Noun + (-chen / -lein)

Base Noun	Suffix	Diminutive	Translation	Notes
Baum	-chen	Bäumchen	little tree	Umlaut added to the base vowel
Haus	-chen	Häuschen	little house	Umlaut added to the base vowel
Kind	-lein	Kindlein	dear little child	*-lein* conveys endearment
Mann	-lein	Männlein	little man	Reflects smallness
Katze	-chen	Kätzchen	kitten	Reflects youngness
Vogel	-chen	Vögelchen	little bird	Reflects smallness

When the intent is to represent the smaller version or a small instance of something, *-chen* is predominantly used. This use is common when referring to objects or animals.

↳ *Hund* → *Hündchen*
(little dog)

The *-lein* suffix is often engaged when the speaker wishes to convey a sense of affection or endearment, usually when referring to people.

↳ *Tochter* → *Töchterlein*
(dear little daughter)

When the diminutive is used to denote a young or infantile version of something, *-chen* is the frequent choice.

↳ *Katze* → *Kätzchen*
(cat, little kitten)

While *-chen* is universally used, the *-lein* suffix is distinctly characteristic of the dialects of Southern Germany. This regional variation enriches the linguistic tapestry of the German language, offering speakers varied avenues to express their feelings and perceptions, aligning with their cultural and geographical identities.

The addition of an *Umlaut* — ä, ö, ü — to the vowel of the base noun is a common alteration when forming diminutives. This modification not only impacts the pronunciation but also adds to the distinctive sound characteristic of diminutives in German.

↳ *Blume* → *Blümchen* (little flower)

It's pivotal to remember that irrespective of the original noun's gender, the derived diminutive is invariably neutral, utilizing the article „das". This neutrality in gender underscores the universality of diminutives in representing objects, animals, and people across gender categories in the German language.

\multicolumn{4}{c}{Diminutive im Deutschen: Verkleinerungsformen und ihre Bedeutungen (German Diminutives: Reduced Forms and Their Meanings)}			
Deutsch	Bedeutung	Beispiel	Bedeutung des Beispiels
Häuschen	kleines Haus	Wir haben ein Häuschen im Wald.	We have a little house in the forest.
Mädchen	junges weibliches Kind	Das Mädchen liest ein Buch.	The young girl is reading a book.
Bäumchen	kleiner Baum	Sie pflanzte ein Bäumchen.	She planted a little tree.
Blümchen	kleine Blume	Auf der Wiese wachsen Blümchen.	Little flowers are growing in the meadow.
Tässchen	kleine Tasse	Ich trinke Kaffee aus einem Tässchen.	I am drinking coffee from a little cup.
Vögelchen	kleiner Vogel	Ein Vögelchen singt im Baum.	A little bird is singing in the tree.
Hündchen	kleiner Hund	Das Hündchen spielt im Garten.	The little dog is playing in the garden.
Büchlein	kleines Buch	Ich lese ein interessantes Büchlein.	I am reading an interesting little book.
Söhnchen	kleiner Sohn	Ihr Söhnchen ist sehr süß.	Her little son is very sweet.
Tischchen	kleiner Tisch	Auf dem Tischchen steht eine Lampe.	There is a lamp on the little table.
Äpfelchen	kleiner Apfel	Ich esse ein süßes Äpfelchen.	I am eating a sweet little apple.

2.5 DERIVATION (DERIVATION)

▷ Ü 2.2), 2.4)

Derivation in the German language is a potent grammatical mechanism that allows for the creation of new words by attaching prefixes, suffixes, or infixes to base words. This linguistic feature significantly broadens the communicative scope of the language, allowing speakers to convey more specific or nuanced meanings, describe new concepts, phenomena, or objects, and enrich the expressivity and adaptive capacity of German.

The formation of derived words in German is fundamentally anchored in the integration of affixes to the root word. The type and meaning of the affix determine the semantic shift or the creation of new semantic dimensions within the derived word.

Base Word	Affix	Derived Word	Translation
singen	be-	besingen	to sing the praises of
Arbeit	-er	Arbeiter	worker
lesen	ver-	sich verlesen	to misread
Lauf	-ig	läufig	in heat (for animals)

Prefixes	Prefixes are placed before the base word to modify its meaning. They can indicate direction, negation, completion, or other nuanced changes in meaning. spielen → vorspielen (to play) (to perform, to audition)
Suffixes	Suffixes are added to the end of the base word and can often change the word class, such as transforming a verb into a noun or an adjective. schnell → Schnelligkeit (fast) (speed, swiftness)

German Made Easy Level 2 | Unit 3

Nomen (Nouns)				
Base Word	**Affix**	**Derived Word**	**Translation**	**Semantic Shift**
Schule	-er	Schüler	student	Person associated with the base word
Arbeit	-er	Arbeiter	worker	Person associated with the base word
Foto	-graf	Fotograf	photographer	Person associated with the object
Auto	-fahrer	Autofahrer	car driver	Person associated with the object
Freund	-schaft	Freundschaft	friendship	State or condition related to the base word
Hand	-schuh	Handschuh	glove	Object associated with the base word
Fuß	-ball	Fußball	football (soccer)	Object associated with the base word
Buch	-handlung	Buchhandlung	bookstore	Place associated with the base word
Wissenschaft	-ler	Wissenschaftler	scientist	Person associated with the base word
Kunst	-ler	Künstler	artist	Person associated with the base word

Verben (Verbs)				
Base Word	Affix	Derived Word	Translation	Semantic Shift
singen	be-	besingen	to sing the praises of	Action is directed towards an object
trinken	ver-	vertrinken	to drink away	Destruction / loss of something through the action.
schreiben	be-	beschreiben	to describe	Creation of something through the action
kaufen	ver-	verkaufen	to sell	Action is directed towards an object
lehren	be-	belehren	to lecture, to instruct	The action is directed towards an object
lernen	er-	erlernen	to learn, to acquire	Acquire knowledge through learning
sehen	be-	besehen	to look at, to view	Action is directed towards an object
denken	nach-	nachdenken	to think over, to reflect	Action becomes deliberate
kommen	an-	ankommen	to arrive	Action is directed towards a goal
machen	auf-	aufmachen	to open	Action is directed towards an object

Adjektive (Adjectives)				
Base Word	Affix	Derived Word	Translation	Semantic Shift
Glück	-lich	glücklich	happy	Describing a state or condition
Farbe	-ig	farbig	colored	Describing a state or condition
Sorge	-los	sorglos	carefree	Describing a state or condition
Punkt	-lich	pünktlich	punctual	Describing a state or condition
Sonne	-ig	sonnig	sunny	Describing a state or condition
Wunder	-bar	wunderbar	wonderful	Describing a state or condition

Nachhaltiges Leben in Deutschland (Sustainable living in Germany) – Wortschatz (Vocabulary)

umweltbewusst [adj.]	environmentally conscious
kompostieren [v.]	(to) compost
reduzieren [v.]	(to) reduce
recyceln [v.]	(to) recycle
nachhaltig [adj.]	sustainable
unterstützen [v.]	(to) support
(das) Fahrrad (Fahrräder) [n.]	bicycle
pflanzen [v.]	(to) plant
öffentlich [adj.]	public
(das) Verkehrsmittel (-) [n.]	means of transportation
frisch [adj.]	fresh
(die) Luft (Lüfte) [n.]	air
(der) Schatten (-) [n.]	shade
(die) Stadt (Städte) [n.]	city
(die) Wichtigkeit (-en) [n.]	importance
(das) Kind (-er) [n.]	child
pflegen [v.]	(to) nurture
entzückend [adj.]	delightful
schätzen [v.]	(to) cherish
(die) Wertschätzung (-en) [n.]	appreciation
beginnen [v.]	(to) begin
anbieten [v.]	(to) offer
umweltfreundlich [adj.]	environmentally friendly
(die) Schule (-n) [n.]	school
(die) Universität (-en) [n.]	university
(das) Projekt (-e) [n.]	project
(die) Initiative (-n) [n.]	initiative
(das) Bewusstsein (-e) [n.]	awareness
beitragen [v.]	(to) contribute
jung [adj.]	young
alt [adj.]	old

Deutschlands Bemühungen um den Umweltschutz
(Germany's efforts in environmental protection) – *Wortschatz* (Vocabulary)

(die) Entwicklung (-en) [n.]	development
(die) Technologie (-n) [n.]	technology
(der) Naturschutz (-e) [n.]	conservation
aktiv [adj.]	active
versuchen [v.]	(to) attempt
groß [adj.]	great
(der) Beitrag (Beiträge) [n.]	contribution
erstaunlich [adj.]	amazing
innovativ [adj.]	innovative
(die) Lösung (-en) [n.]	solution
(der) Planet (-en) [n.]	planet
schützen [v.]	(to) protect
erneuerbar [adj.]	renewable
(die) Energie (-n) [n.]	energy
investieren [v.]	(to) invest
(die) Windkraft (Windkräfte) [n.]	wind power
(die) Solarenergie (-n) [n.]	solar energy
(der) Bienenstock (Bienenstöcke) [n.]	beehive
installieren [v.]	(to) install
wunderbar [adj.]	wonderful
(der) Unterschied (-e) [n.]	difference
(die) Ableitung (-en) [n.]	derivation
(die) Methode (-n) [n.]	method
(die) Tierwelt (-en) [n.]	wildlife
(die) Bemühung (-en) [n.]	effort
vorbildlich [adj.]	exemplary
einsetzen [v.]	(to) employ
lebenswert [adj.]	liveable
(die) Generation (-en) [n.]	generation

Section 3
DIE DEUTSCHE TIERWELT ENTDECKEN
(DISCOVERING GERMAN WILDLIFE)

 SELTENE TIERE IN DEUTSCHLAND
(RARE ANIMALS IN GERMANY)

Jakob and Johanna discuss the existence and characteristics of rare animals in Germany, illustrating the use of German particles and relative clauses without prepositions to describe their fascination and concern for these unique species.

Jakob: Hast du **schon mal** von dem seltenen Luchs in Deutschland gehört?

Johanna: Ja, **doch**, ich habe **mal** darüber gelesen! Es ist **sehr** interessant, dass es hier Tiere gibt, die man kaum **sieht**.

Jakob: **Ziemlich** faszinierend, **nicht wahr**? Es gibt auch Wölfe, die in den Wäldern leben.

Johanna: **Wirklich**? Ich dachte, Wölfe **seien** hier **ziemlich** rar.

Jakob: Ja, **tatsächlich**. Es sind allerdings nachtaktive Tiere, **die** in abgelegenen Gebieten leben.

Johanna: Und es gibt **auch** Fledermäuse, **nicht**? Ich habe gehört, dass es Arten gibt, **die** man **nur** hier findet.

Jakob: Genau, es ist **doch wirklich** eine Schande, dass viele von ihnen bedroht sind.

Johanna: **Ja**, es ist **sehr** wichtig, dass wir mehr tun, um diese Tiere zu schützen, **die** einen wichtigen Teil unseres Ökosystems darstellen.

Jakob: Absolut, es sind **ja** diese speziellen Arten, **die** unsere Natur **so** einzigartig und vielfältig machen.

BESUCH IM DEUTSCHEN ZOO (VISIT TO THE GERMAN ZOO)

Anna and David visit a German zoo, expressing their excitement and observations using different particles and discussing the animals they see using relative clauses without prepositions.

Anna: Oh, sieh **mal**, David! Da sind die Elefanten, die wir schon **so** lange sehen **wollten**!

David: Ja, **stimmt**! Und schau, da ist ein Babyelefant, der **ziemlich** süß aussieht!

Anna: Ja, Elefanten sind **wirklich** faszinierend! Aber wo sind denn die Affen, die immer **so** lustig sind?

David: Ich denke, sie sind gleich dort drüben in diesem Bereich. Wir sollten **doch mal** dort vorbeischauen!

Anna: **Gute Idee**! Ich hoffe, wir sehen die kleinen Äffchen, die **immer so** viel Unsinn machen!

David: Oh, und dort sind die Zebras mit ihren Streifen! Hast du **schon mal** ein Zebra von so **nah** gesehen?

Anna: Nein, noch **nie**! Es ist **wirklich** ein interessanter Tag, **nicht wahr**?

David: Ja, **wirklich**! Ich bin froh, dass wir den Zoo besucht haben, der **so viele** verschiedene Tiere hat!

3.1 PARTIKELN (PARTICLES)

The German language harbors a fascinating grammatical component known as „*Partikeln*" or particles in English. These intricate elements, though seemingly minor, play a monumental role in enriching the semantic texture of a conversation, modifying the mood, tone, or nuance of a sentence or word. Unlike conventional lexical elements, particles do not possess a concrete grammatical function nor do they have direct English translations, making them elusive to non-native speakers. Here, we will delve deeper into the varied types of particles, exploring their functionalities and manifestations in everyday German communication.

ⓘ GUT ZU WISSEN

Germany, Austria, and Switzerland are blessed with diverse habitats, from alpine meadows to dense forests, which are home to a great variety of creatures. Germany's Black Forest is renowned for its lynx and wild boars. Austria's National Park Gesäuse is a haven for golden eagles and marmots. Switzerland, with its high-altitude landscapes, is home to the iconic ibex and the elusive snow hare.

3.1.1 MODALPARTIKELN (MODAL PARTICLES)

Modal particles, such as „doch" and „mal", are intricate components of German linguistic structure. They lend sentences a distinctive emotional color, indicating the speaker's attitude or mood, and subtly altering the listener's comprehension or response to the statement.

Oh, sieh mal, David!
(Oh, look, David!)

Ja, stimmt doch!
(Yes, that's right!)

The application of modal particles reveals a layer of emotion, doubt, surprise, or certainty within a statement. Their deployment is highly context-sensitive, enabling the conveyance of nuanced emotional states and attitudes, providing a glimpse into the speaker's perspective or internal emotional landscape. They are pivotal in expressing a range of emotions and attitudes, allowing for a more expressive, nuanced communication style that is deeply intertwined with the cultural and conversational norms of German-speaking societies.

3.1.2 GRADPARTIKELN (DEGREE PARTICLES)

Degree particles, notably „*sehr*" and „*ziemlich*", serve as modifying agents that elucidate the intensity, degree, or extent of adjectives, adverbs, or other elements within the sentence.

...der ziemlich süß aussieht!
(...that looks quite cute!)

Es war ein sehr interessanter Tag.
(It was a really interesting day.)

Degree particles act as quantifiers, introducing a level of precision and specificity in describing the scale or magnitude of attributes, actions, or states. By incorporating these particles, speakers can portray a more detailed, accurate picture of the described phenomena, adjusting the emphasis according to the contextual needs and communicative intentions, thus allowing a clearer, more detailed depiction of one's observations or perceptions.

3.1.3 ANTWORTPARTIKELN (RESPONSE PARTICLES)

Response particles like „*ja*" and „*nein*" are succinct expressions employed to deliver clear, unambiguous affirmations or negations to statements, propositions, or inquiries.

Ja, stimmt doch!
(Yes, that's right!)

Nein, noch nie!
(No, never before!)

The use of response particles exemplifies the efficiency of German communication. They are clear, concise, and leave no ambiguity in conveying agreement, acceptance, refusal, or denial, enhancing the fluidity and coherence of conversational exchanges by providing straightforward, unambiguous reactions to preceding utterances.

3.1.4 NEGATIONSPARTIKELN (NEGATION PARTICLES)

„*Nicht*", the negation particle, is integral in German syntax, serving to negate various sentence elements, thus asserting the non-occurrence, absence, or opposition of the stated actions, qualities, or entities.

... der nicht so weit von hier ist.
(...which is not so far from here.)

The employment of „*nicht*" brings a dimension of assertiveness and contradiction to German sentences. It distinctly denotes the opposite of a given statement, emphasizing the absence or non-occurrence of actions, attributes, or objects, thereby providing a counterbalance to affirmative statements and enriching the expressive versatility of the language.

Type	Examples	Purpose	Usage	Example Sentence
Modalpartikeln	eben, ja	Modify mood, express attitude or emotion.	Used to convey surprise, doubt, certainty, or emotion.	*Das ist ja interessant!* (That is indeed interesting!)
Gradpartikeln	etwas, voll	Quantify or modify intensity or degree.	Provide information about the degree of attributes or actions.	*Das ist etwas kompliziert.* (That is somewhat complicated.)
Antwortpartikeln	doch, wohl	Convey agreement or denial.	Quick responses to affirm or negate statements or questions.	*Du kommst doch, oder etwa nicht?* (You are coming, aren't you?)
Negationspartikel	kein	Assert non-occurrence or absence.	Used to negate verbs, adjectives, nouns, etc.	*Das ist kein Problem.* (That is not a problem.)

3.2 DIE INDIREKTE REDE (REPORTED SPEECH)

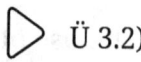 Ü 3.2)

Indirekte Rede (Reported Speech) is a pivotal element in the German language, allowing speakers to relay or report the speech, thoughts, or expressions of a person in a manner that is not a direct quotation. It is significant in a variety of contexts, enabling the conveyance of information, narratives, and perspectives in a seamless and cohesive manner.

When transforming direct speech into reported speech in German, verb tenses, pronouns, and time expressions are typically adjusted to align with the context and perspective of the reporting speaker. Additionally, it usually necessitates the use of *Konjunktiv I* (Subjunctive I) for the verb to maintain a sense of uncertainty or indirectness, ensuring that the speech reported is distinguished from the direct quotation.

Direct Speech	Reported Speech
Lisa sagt: „Ich habe ein Reh gesehen." (Lisa says, "I have seen a deer.")	*Lisa sagt, sie habe ein Reh gesehen.* ("Lisa says that she had seen a deer.")

3.2.1 TRANSFORMATION PATTERN (TRANSFORMATION PATTERN)

- **Conjugate Verb in *Konjunktiv I***
  The transition from direct to reported speech often requires modifications in verb tenses to depict the temporality of the reported action or state appropriately. Additionally, verbs are usually conjugated in *Konjunktiv I* to denote the indirect, reported nature of the speech.

  ↳ **Direct:** „Ich gehe zum Markt."
  (I am going to the market.)

  Reported: *Er sagt, er gehe zum Markt.*
  (He says he is going to the market.)

- **Adjust Pronouns**
  Pronouns in reported speech need to be adapted to align with the reporting speaker's perspective, ensuring cohesion and clarity in the relayed message.

  ↳ **Direct:** „Du hast das Buch."
  (You have the book.)

  Reported: *Sie sagt, ich hätte das Buch.*
  (She says I have the book.)

- **Modify Time Expressions if Necessary**
  The reported speech must be harmoniously woven into the broader narrative or conversation, reflecting the accurate conveyance of thoughts, emotions, and information.

  ↳ **Direct:** „Wir werden morgen ankommen."
  (We will arrive tomorrow.)

  Reported: *Er meint, sie würden morgen ankommen.*
  (He thinks they will arrive tomorrow.)

3.3 KONJUNKTIV (SUBJUNCTIVE)

3.3.1 KONJUNKTIV I (SUBJUNCTIVE I) ▷ Ü 3.3

Konjunktiv I (Subjunctive I) is an integral mood in German grammar used primarily to convey reported speech, hypothetical situations, and to express wishes, doubt, or indirect queries. It is quintessential for establishing a sense of indirection or unreality, distinguishing the content from factual statements, and embedding nuanced layers of meaning in communication.

Konjunktiv I is primarily formed by taking the stem of the verb from the present tense and adding specific endings, typically involving *-e, -est, -e, -en, -et, -en*. However, for many verbs, particularly in the singular form, *Konjunktiv I* can resemble the indicative mood, leading to the use of *würde* (would) to avoid ambiguity.

Formation Pattern	
Infinitive	haben
Stem	hab-
Konjunktiv I	ich habe, du habest, er/sie/es habe, wir haben, ihr habet, sie/Sie haben

Konjunktiv I is extensively used to express reported speech, allowing the speaker to convey statements, thoughts, or expressions made by others in an indirect manner.

Direct: *Sie sagt: „Ich bin müde."* (She says, "I'm tired.")
Reported: *Sie sagt, sie sei müde.* ("She says that she is tired.")

It can be employed to articulate wishes, hopes, and polite requests, imbuing the conversation with a tone of courtesy and formality.

↳ *Möge das Glück mit dir sein!* (May luck be with you!)

Konjunktiv I serves to express uncertainty, doubt, or speculative situations, thus distinguishing the content from factual or declarative statements.

↳ *Es sei möglich, dass er kommt.* (It is possible that he comes.)

Aspect	Description	Example	Detailed Examination
Reported Speech	Relays statements, thoughts, or expressions indirectly.	*Sie meint, es sei zu spät.* (She believes that it was too late.)	Distinguishes the reported content from direct quotations.
Expressing Wishes	Articulates hopes, wishes, and polite requests.	*Mögest du glücklich sein!* (May you be happy!)	Provides a tone of courtesy and formality in the communication.
Indicating Doubt	Depicts uncertainty, doubt, or speculative situations.	*Es könnte regnerisch sein.* (It might be rainy.)	Differentiates speculative or uncertain content from factual statements.

3.3.2 KONJUNKTIV II
(SUBJUNCTIVE II)

The *Konjunktiv II*, or Subjunctive II is used in German grammar to express unrealistic, hypothetical, untrue, or desired conditions. When constructing conditional sentences, expressing unrealizable desires, and describing hypothetical situations, it is of paramount importance. It serves as an invaluable tool for expressing the subtleties of emotion, conditionality, and improbability.

Konjunktiv II is formed by modifying the stem of the verbs, predominantly in the preterite, and appending specific endings. For regular verbs, it retains the preterite form, while irregular verbs often undergo umlaut changes and adopt *"würden"* + infinitive constructions to avoid ambiguity.

Formation Pattern	
Infinitive	*gehen*
Stem	*ging-*
Konjunktiv II	*ich ginge, du gingest, er/sie/es ginge, wir gingen, ihr ginget, sie/Sie gingen*

Konjunktiv II is essential for constructing conditional sentences to express hypothetical situations and their imagined or desired outcomes.

> *Wenn ich reich wäre, würde ich ein Haus kaufen.*
> (If I were rich, I would buy a house.)

It serves to articulate desires, wishes, and hopes that are unattainable or yet to be realized, rendering a touch of longing or wistfulness to the expression.

> *Ich wünschte, ich hätte mehr Zeit.*
> (I wish I had more time.)

It can be employed to frame requests, offers, and suggestions politely and subtly, emphasizing courtesy and considerateness in interaction.

> *Könnten Sie mir bitte helfen?*
> (Could you please help me?)

Aspect	Description	Example	Detailed Examination
Conditional Sentences	Creates hypothetical scenarios and their possible outcomes.	*Wenn er schneller liefe, würde er gewinnen.* (If he ran faster, he would win.)	Details situations that are speculative, hypothetical, or unattained.
Expressing Wishes	Articulates unattainable desires, hopes, and wishes.	*Ich wünschte, ich könnte fliegen.* (I wish I could fly.)	Adds a layer of wistfulness, longing, or regret to the conversation.
Polite Requests	Frames polite, subtle requests, offers, and suggestions.	*Würden Sie mir das Salz reichen?* (Would you pass me the salt?)	Emphasizes courtesy, consideration, and politeness in interactions.

Besuch im Deutschen Zoo (Visit to the German Zoo)	
German	English
(der) Zoo	zoo
(das) Gehege	enclosure
(der) Elefant	elephant
füttern	(to) feed
beobachten	(to) observe
(das) Raubtier	predator
(der) Pflanzenfresser	herbivore
(der) Löwe	lion
(die) Schlange	snake
interaktiv	interactive
lehrreich	educational
(die) Tierpflegerin	zookeeper (female)
(der) Affe	monkey
(die) Giraffe	giraffe
(die) Führung	tour

Outdoor-Aktivitäten (Outdoor Activities)	
German	English
wandern	(to) hike
zelten	(to) camp
angeln	(to) fish
klettern	(to) climb
Fußball spielen	(to) play soccer/football
Rad fahren	(to) cycle
schwimmen	(to) swim
tauchen	(to) dive
surfen	(to) surf
segeln	(to) sail
Ski fahren	(to) ski
Snowboard fahren	(to) snowboard
Kayak fahren	(to) kayak
Rafting	(to) go rafting
joggen	(to) jog
spazieren gehen	(to) go for a walk
Picknick machen	(to) have a picnic
Vögel beobachten	(to) go bird watching
fotografieren	(to) photograph
Bergsteigen	(to) mountaineer
Drachen steigen lassen	(to) fly a kite

ÜBUNGEN (EXERCISES)

Ü 1.1) Fülle die Tabelle aus, indem du das korrekte reflexive Verb und das passende reflexive Pronomen einsetzt. Beachte dabei die richtige Konjugation des Verbs.
Fill in the table by inserting the correct reflexive verb and the matching reflexive pronoun. Pay attention to the correct conjugation of the verb.

Example:

Subjekt	Reflexives Verb	Reflexives Pronomen	Übersetzung
ich	freue	mich	I am looking forward to

Verwende das Verb „sich vergewissern" und fülle die Tabelle aus.
Use the verb „sich vergewissern" and complete the table.

Subjekt	Reflexives Verb	Reflexives Pronomen	Übersetzung
du		dich	
er		sich	
sie (feminin)		sich	
wir		uns	
ihr		euch	
sie (plural)		sich	
Sie (Höflichkeitsform)		sich	

Ü 2.1) Lies die Sätze und setze in die Lücken die korrekte Form des Verbs im Infinitiv mit „zu" ein. Achte darauf, dass der Satz sinnvoll ist.
Read the sentences and fill in the blanks with the correct form of the verb in the infinitive with „zu". Make sure that the sentence makes sense.

Example: Es ist nicht einfach _____ (lernen) → Es ist nicht einfach, zu lernen.

a. Er hat vergessen _____ (einkaufen), deshalb haben wir nichts zum Abendessen.

b. Ich freue mich darauf, dich _____ (sehen).

c. Sie versucht, den Text _____ (verstehen).

d. Wir haben beschlossen, früh _____ (aufstehen).

e. Es ist oft schwer, die Wahrheit _____ (sagen).

f. Die Kinder haben angefangen, _____ (weinen), weil sie müde waren.

g. Ich brauche eine Pause, um wieder zu Atem _____ (kommen).

h. Es ist gefährlich, ohne Helm _____ (fahren).

i. Wir planen, nächstes Jahr nach Deutschland _____ (reisen).

j. Sie hofft, bald einen neuen Job _____ (finden).

Ü 2.2) Schau dir die Bilder an und schreibe das passende Diminutiv zu jedem Bild. Denke daran, dass Diminutive oft durch die Endungen „-chen" oder „-lein" gebildet werden, um etwas als kleiner oder lieblicher darzustellen.

Look at the pictures and write the corresponding diminutive for each image. Remember that diminutives are often formed by adding the suffixes „-chen" or „-lein" to depict something as smaller or more endearing.

Example:

H<u>u</u>nd
↓
H<u>ü</u>nd**chen**

a. **b.** **c.** **d.**

↓ ↓ ↓ ↓

e. _____ f. _____ g. _____ h. _____
↓ ↓ ↓ ↓
_____ _____ _____ _____

Ü 2.3) Bilde abgeleitete Wörter durch Hinzufügen von Präfixen und/oder Suffixen und fülle die Tabelle aus.

Form derived words by adding prefixes and/or suffixes and complete the table.

Example:

Basiswort (Base Word)	Mit Präfix (With Prefix)	Mit Suffix (With Suffix)	Mit Präfix und Suffix (With Prefix and Suffix)
Glück	Unglück	Glücklichkeit	Unglücklichkeit

Basiswort (Base Word)	Mit Präfix (With Prefix)	Mit Suffix (With Suffix)	Mit Präfix und Suffix (With Prefix and Suffix)
Freund			
leben			
trinken			
schreib			
Spiel			
laufen			
sehen			
arbeiten			

Ü 2.4) Finde die passenden Wortfamilien. Schreibe das Basiswort und dann alle davon abgeleiteten Wörter, die dir einfallen, in die Tabelle.

Find the matching word families. Write the base word and then all the words that are derived from it in the table.

Example:

Basiswort (Base Word)	Abgeleitete Wörter (Derived Words)
Glück	Glücklichkeit, glücklich, unglücklich, Unglück

Basiswort (Base Word)	Abgeleitete Wörter (Derived Words)
Trinken	
Schreiben	
Sicht	
Hören	
Bild	
Lernen	
Verstand	
Schlaf	
Fahren	
Lesen	
Bau	
Glauben	
Spiel	

Ü 3.1) Verbinde die Sätze oder Satzteile mit der passenden Partikel. Achte darauf, dass die Partikel inhaltlich und kontextuell zum Satz passt.
Connect the sentences or parts of sentences with the appropriate particle. Make sure that the particle is contextually and content-wise suitable for the sentence.

Example: „Du kommst morgen _____ , oder?" •————————————• doch

a. „Das ist _____ eine gute Idee!" •

b. „Könntest du das _____ erklären?" •

c. „Er spielt _____ gut Klavier." •

d. „Wir gehen jetzt _____ nach Hause." •

e. „Das schmeckt _____ lecker!" •

f. „Du bist _____ gekommen." •

g. „Mach das _____ auf!" •

h. „Das wird _____ interessant." •

i. „Sie hat _____ ja gesagt." •

j. „Kommst du _____ mit?" •

• mal

• sehr

• doch

• ziemlich

• nicht

• ja

• nein

Ü 3.2) Wandle die direkten Reden in indirekte Reden um. Achte darauf, dass du die richtige Konjugation der Verben und die korrekten Pronomen verwendest.
Transform the direct speeches into reported speeches. Ensure that you use the correct conjugation of the verbs and the correct pronouns.

Example: *Direkte Rede:* Er sagt: „Ich habe das Buch gelesen."
             Indirekte Rede: Er sagt, er habe das Buch gelesen.

a. Sie sagt: „Ich werde morgen kommen."

_____

b. Er sagt: „Ich kann das nicht machen."

_____

c. Wir sagen: „Wir sind im Kino."

_____

d. Du sagst: „Ich habe Hunger."

e. Sie (Plural) sagen: „Wir werden das Projekt beenden."

f. Ich sage: „Ich gehe spazieren."

g. Ihr sagt: „Wir haben das Spiel gewonnen."

h. Er sagt: „Ich werde das Auto reparieren."

i. Sie sagt: „Ich kann das Fenster öffnen."

j. Du sagst: „Ich will ein Eis essen."

Ü 3.3) Vervollständige die Sätze mit der passenden Form des Verbs im Konjunktiv I. Achte darauf, das Verb in der korrekten Person und Numerus zu konjugieren.

Complete the sentences with the appropriate form of the verb in Subjunctive I. Make sure to conjugate the verb in the correct person and number.

Example: Er sagt, er **(sein)** zu Hause. ⟶ Er sagt, er **sei** zu Hause.

a. Sie behauptet, sie (haben) keine Zeit.

b. Er meint, er (können) das nicht machen.

c. Wir denken, wir (müssen) früher aufstehen.

d. Du sagst, du (wollen) das Buch lesen.

e. Ich habe gehört, ich (sollen) Sie anrufen.

f. Sie erklären, es (sein) wichtig.

g. Er glaubt, er (werden) gewinnen.

h. Wir vermuten, ihr (mögen) keinen Kaffee. _____

i. Sie denkt, sie (können) das lösen. _____

j. Ich sage, du (liegen) richtig. _____

Ü 3.4) Formuliere die Sätze so um, dass sie einen Wunsch oder eine Hypothese mit Konjunktiv II ausdrücken.

Rephrase the sentences so that they express a wish or a hypothesis using Subjunctive II.

Example: Ich lerne mehr. → Ich würde mehr lernen.

a. Du gehst früher. _____

b. Er findet die Lösung. _____

c. Wir reisen nach Deutschland. _____

d. Ihr spielt im Park. _____

e. Sie (Singular, feminin) kocht Abendessen. _____

f. Es regnet. _____

g. Ich antworte. _____

h. Sie (Plural) sehen den Film. _____

i. Du singst ein Lied. _____

j. Er spricht Spanisch. _____

Unit 4

REISEN UND ABENTEUER

(TRAVEL AND ADVENTURE)

In Unit IV, „*Reisen und Abenteuer*", you'll explore the German language through the exciting lens of travel and adventure. The unit starts with „*Reiseplanung*", where you'll learn specific language constructs for planning and discussing travel, including future tense usage and conditional phrases. This section helps you navigate through various travel-related scenarios, using language as a tool to articulate plans and possibilities. In „*Reiseziele*", the focus shifts to discussing different travel destinations, employing rich vocabulary and complex sentence structures to describe various cultural and geographical landscapes. The unit culminates with „*Unvergessliche Reiseerlebnisse teilen*", aimed at enhancing your ability to share travel experiences, focusing on time expressions, idiomatic phrases, and narrative structures. This unit is not just about language learning; it's a journey through the diverse and exciting world of travel, using German as a medium to explore and share experiences.

Section 1

REISEPLANUNG
(TRAVEL PLANNING)

 TRAUMURLAUB AM HORIZONT
(DREAM VACATION ON THE HORIZON)

Johannes and Sabrina are sitting at a café, excitedly discussing plans for their upcoming dream vacation.

Johannes: Sabrina, **wenn** wir genug Geld sparen, sollten wir wirklich nach Bali fliegen. Es ist mein Traum, dort zu surfen.

Sabrina: Das klingt großartig, **sobald** wir alles geplant haben, kann es losgehen. Ich habe gehört, dass die Strände dort atemberaubend sind. Aber **falls** es regnet, sollten wir auch einige Indoor-Aktivitäten im Hinterkopf behalten.

Johannes: Gute Idee. **Lassen** wir uns von einem Reisebüro beraten. Sie könnten uns gute Empfehlungen geben.

Sabrina: Ja, und vielleicht könnten sie uns auch dabei helfen, einige Ausflüge zu buchen. Ich möchte unbedingt die Reisterrassen **besichtigen**.

Johannes: Das klingt nach einem Plan! Ich freue mich darauf, den ganzen Tag am Strand zu **sonnenbaden** und abends in einem der Strandrestaurants zu essen.

Sabrina: Ich auch. Und **lassen** wir uns auf jeden Fall eine balinesische Massage geben. Das wäre die perfekte Entspannung.

Johannes: Definitiv! Und **falls** wir noch Zeit haben, könnten wir einen Kochkurs machen und lernen, wie man traditionelle balinesische Gerichte **zubereitet**.

Sabrina: Ja, das klingt nach einer super Idee! **Lassen** wir uns überraschen, was Bali alles für uns bereithält!

DIE SCHÖNHEIT DES REISENS
(THE BEAUTY OF TRAVEL)

Das Reisen öffnet nicht nur die Türen zu neuen Orten, sondern auch zu neuen Erfahrungen und Perspektiven. **Wenn** *man eine neue Stadt besucht, entdeckt man oft unerwartete Schätze, sei es in Form von Architektur, Kunst oder sogar lokalen Traditionen. Es ist eine Sache, über einen Ort zu lesen, und eine ganz andere, ihn selbst zu erleben.*

Manchmal **lässt** *uns ein einfacher Spaziergang durch eine unbekannte Straße unsere Vorstellungen und Überzeugungen hinterfragen. Und* **falls** *du die Gelegenheit* **hast***, mit Einheimischen zu sprechen, wirst du feststellen, dass trotz unserer Unterschiede, die Menschheit viele Gemeinsamkeiten hat.*

Das Beste am Reisen ist jedoch das Unerwartete. **Sobald** *wir unsere Komfortzone verlassen, sind wir offen für Abenteuer. Es* **lässt** *sich* **nicht** *voraussagen, was hinter der nächsten Ecke wartet. Und manchmal sind es die kleinen Dinge, die am meisten beeindrucken, wie das* **Zusammensitzen** *mit neuen Freunden unter einem sternenklaren Himmel oder der Abstand von der Hektik des Alltags und das* **Eintauchen** *in eine andere Kultur.*

Reisen lehrt uns, mit offenen Augen und Herzen durch die Welt zu gehen. Es ist ein Geschenk, das uns erlaubt, die Welt und uns selbst aus einem neuen Blickwinkel zu betrachten.

🛈 GUT ZU WISSEN

When exploring the German-speaking countries, each offers a distinctive charm. In Germany, consider a visit to Neuschwanstein Castle in Schwangau, not just for its fairy-tale appeal, but also for the breathtaking landscapes surrounding it. If you're venturing by car, don't miss out on the "Romantic Road" between Salzburg and Vienna for a picturesque drive. For music lovers, Austria is a haven. Salzburg, Mozart's birthplace, offers musical tours and events year-round. Meanwhile, Vienna's opera is a must-experience. In Switzerland, try to travel by train; their rail system is not only efficient but provides some of Europe's most captivating panoramic views. If you're there during winter, the Swiss Alps are a skiing paradise, and in summer, they turn into perfect hiking terrains.

1.1 DIE VERWENDUNG VON „WENN", „FALLS", „SOBALD"
(USAGE OF „WENN", „FALLS", „SOBALD")

Understanding how to use „wenn", „falls", and „sobald" is essential in the German language. These conjunctions help express conditions, assumptions, or denote the time of occurrence of an action.

„wenn"

↳ The German word „wenn" can be translated as "if" or "when" in English, depending on the context.

It is used to refer to:

- Conditional situations
- Repeated events or habitual actions in the past
- Direct or indirect questions

„falls"

↳ „Falls" can be translated as "in case" or "if". It is primarily used to express a condition, often implying a degree of uncertainty.

„sobald"

↳ „Sobald" means "as soon as" in English. It is used to indicate the exact time when an action will take place.

Conjunction	Function	Example Sentence	Translation
wenn	Conditional	*Wenn* es regnet, bleiben wir zu Hause.	If it rains, we stay at home.
	Repeated events/ habitual actions in the past	*Wenn* ich als Kind krank war, las mir meine Mutter vor.	As a child, when I was sick, my mother used to read to me.
	Direct/Indirect questions	Weißt du, was passiert, *wenn* das Konzert beginnt?	Do you know what happens when the concert starts?
falls	Conditional with uncertainty	*Falls* du Hunger hast, gibt es noch Kuchen in der Küche.	In case you are hungry, there's still some cake in the kitchen.
sobald	Indicating exact time of action	Ich werde dich anrufen, *sobald* ich zu Hause bin.	I will call you as soon as I get home.

1.2 DER GEBRAUCH VON „LASSEN" (USING „LASSEN")

The verb „lassen" is versatile and is used in a variety of contexts, ranging from permitting or allowing something to occur, to having something done by someone else. Let's understand the different ways in which „lassen" is utilized:

1. **Permitting or Allowing**
In this context, „lassen" means to let or allow someone to do something.

Ich lasse ihn gehen.
(I let him go.)

2. **To Have Something Done**
„lassen" can also be used to indicate that someone is having something done by someone else. It often denotes that the subject is not performing the action directly but is instead getting it done through another person.

Ich lasse mein Auto reparieren.
(I am getting my car repaired.)

3. **Requests or Suggestions**
When used in a more informal context, „lassen" can be a way to make a request or offer a suggestion.

Lass uns ins Kino gehen!
(Let's go to the cinema!)

4. **To Leave Something As It Is**
„lassen" can also mean to leave something in a particular state or condition.

Lass das Fenster offen.
(Leave the window open.)

5. **In Combination With Another Verb**
„lassen" can combine with another verb to form a unique meaning. This is similar to the English "let".

Er lässt sich nicht stören.
(He won't let himself be disturbed.)

1.3 GETRENNT- UND ZUSAMMENSCHREIBUNG
(SEPARATION AND COMPOUNDING)

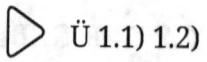

In German, compound words are a crucial aspect of vocabulary. However, deciding when to write words separately (*Getrenntschreibung*) or together (*Zusammenschreibung*) can be challenging.

Zusammenschreibung **(Compounding)**

↳ Compounding creates new words that are often quite long, but specific in meaning.

Verb + Noun
When <u>verbs</u> and <u>nouns</u> come together and produce a meaning that's distinct from the sum of their parts, the resulting compound is typically written as one word.
Lebenslauf (<u>Leben</u> + <u>Lauf</u>)   Staubsauger (<u>Staub</u> + <u>saugen</u>) Resume/CV (to live + Course)   Vacuum cleaner (Dust + to suck)

Noun + Noun
Compounding two nouns can provide a more precise description of an object or concept.
Wasserkocher (Wasser + Kocher)   Handschuh (Hand + Schuh) Kettle (Water + Stove)   Glove (Hand + Shoe)

Adjective + Noun
These compounds describe a particular type of an object.
rothaarig (<u>rot</u> + <u>Haar</u>)   langweilig (<u>lang</u> + <u>Weile</u>) red-haired (red + hair)   boring (long + while)

Getrenntschreibung **(Separation)**

↳ This aspect of the German language often contrasts with compounding and refers to instances where words are written separately.

Verb + Verb
These combinations remain separate, especially when indicating a sequence of actions.
schlafen gehen   arbeiten lernen (to) go to sleep   (to) learn to work

Adjective + Verb
The <u>verb</u> and <u>adjective</u> maintain their distinct roles in the sentence and aren't merged.   <u>krank</u> <u>werden</u>   <u>alt</u> <u>aussehen</u>   (to) become sick   (to) look old

One of the challenging aspects is with prefixed verbs. Some <u>prefixes</u> can lead to *Zusammenschreibung*, while others can lead to *Getrenntschreibung*. Recognizing and understanding these can be particularly important for learners.

<u>herunter</u>laden (herunter + laden)
(download)

<u>vorbei</u>gehen (vorbei + gehen)
(to pass by)

Reisevorbereitungen (Travel Preparations)	
packen	(to) pack
(der) Reisepass	passport
(die) Karte	map
buchen	(to) book
(der) Flug	flight
planen	(to) plan
(die) Tasche	bag
reisen	(to) travel
(der) Zug	train
kaufen	(to) buy
(die) Fahrkarte	ticket (for transportation)
bestätigen	(to) confirm
(der) Koffer	suitcase
vorbereiten	(to) prepare
(das) Gepäck	luggage

Unterkunft (Accommodation)	
(das) Hotel	hotel
(die) Jugendherberge	youth hostel
(die) Pension	bed and breakfast
mieten	(to) rent
(das) Zimmer	room
schlafen	(to) sleep
(der) Gast	guest
reservieren	(to) reserve
(der) Preis	price
(die) Nacht	night
(die) Rezeption	reception
(der) Schlüssel	key
(das) Bad	bathroom
zahlen	(to) pay
(die) Reservierung	reservation

Traumurlaub am Horizont (Dream Vacation on the Horizon) – *Wortschatz* (Vocabulary)

(das) Geld (-er) [n.]	money
sparen [v.]	(to) save
fliegen [v.]	(to) fly
(der) Traum (Träume) [n.]	dream
surfen [v.]	(to) surf
großartig [adj.]	great
planen [v.]	(to) plan
(der) Strand (Strände) [n.]	beach
(die) Aktivität (-en) [n.]	activity
im Hinterkopf behalten [adv.]	(to) keep in mind
(das) Reisebüro (-s) [n.]	travel agency
atemberaubend [adj.]	breathtaking
beraten [v.]	(to) advise
(die) Empfehlung (-en) [n.]	recommendation
helfen [v.]	(to) help
(der) Ausflug (Ausflüge) [n.]	excursion
sonnenbaden [v.]	(to) sunbathing
(die) Reisterrasse (-n) [n.]	rice terrace
buchen [v.]	(to) book
abends [adv.]	in the evening
besichtigen [v.]	(to) visit
(der) Strand (Strände) [n.]	beach
perfekt [adj.]	perfect
(die) Entspannung (-en) [n.]	relaxation
(der) Kochkurs (-e) [n.]	cooking class
traditionell [adj.]	traditional
balinesisch [adj.]	Balinese
zubereiten [v.]	(to) prepare
bereithalten [v.]	(to) have ready

Die Schönheit des Reisens (The Beauty of Travel) – *Wortschatz* (Vocabulary)

(der) Ort (-e) [n.]	place
(die) Perspektive (-n) [n.]	perspective
besuchen [v.]	(to) visit
entdecken [v.]	(to) discover
unerwartet [adj.]	unexpected
(der) Schatz (Schätze) [n.]	treasure
(die) Form (-en) [n.]	form
(die) Architektur (-en) [n.]	architecture
erleben [v.]	(to) experience
(der) Spaziergang (Spaziergänge) [n.]	walk
(die) Vorstellung (-en) [n.]	imagination
(die) Überzeugung (-en) [n.]	conviction
feststellen [v.]	(to) ascertain
(die) Gemeinsamkeit (-en) [n.]	commonality
sobald [conj.]	as soon as
(die) Komfortzone (-n) [n.]	comfort zone
verlassen [v.]	(to) leave
offen [adj.]	open
voraussagen [v.]	(to) predict
(die) Ecke (-n) [n.]	corner
beeindrucken [v.]	(to) impress
zusammensitzen [v.]	(to) sit together
sternenklar [adj.]	starry
(der) Himmel (-) [n.]	sky
(die) Hektik (-) [n.]	bustle
eintauchen [v.]	(to) immerse
(der) Blickwinkel (-) [n.]	perspective / point of view
lehren [v.]	(to) teach
erlauben [v.]	(to) allow

Section 2
REISEZIELE (TRAVEL DESTINATIONS)

 REISEEMPFEHLUNGEN FÜR DEUTSCHLAND
(TRAVEL RECOMMENDATIONS FOR GERMANY)

Wilhelm, an enthusiastic globetrotter, gives Gina, who wants to visit Germany for the first time, some tips and recommendations.

Wilhelm: *Gina, ich bin so froh, dass du dich für Deutschland als Reiseziel entschieden hast! Es gibt dort so viele schöne Orte.*

Gina: *Das habe ich gehört! Aber ich bin mir nicht sicher, wo ich anfangen soll. Ich liebe historische Städte und gutes Essen.* **Obwohl** *ich nur zwei Wochen Zeit habe, möchte ich so viel wie möglich sehen.*

Wilhelm: **Trotzdem** *ist es möglich, einige Highlights zu erleben. Wenn du historische Städte magst, solltest du unbedingt Heidelberg, Rothenburg ob der Tauber und Dresden besuchen. Und was das Essen angeht? Schwierig zu sagen,* **denn** *Deutschland hat eine Vielfalt von regionalen Spezialitäten zu bieten!*

Gina: *Das klingt fantastisch! Aber wie komme ich von einer Stadt zur nächsten? Ich habe gehört, dass die Zugverbindungen ziemlich gut sind.*

Wilhelm: *Na ja, plane am besten etwas mehr Zeit ein, aber* **wenn** *du im Voraus buchst, kannst du wirklich gute Angebote finden.*

Gina: *Was ist mit der Sprachbarriere? Mein Deutsch ist nicht das Beste.* **Wenn** *ich fließend sprechen könnte,* **würde** *ich mich wahrscheinlich wohler fühlen.*

Wilhelm: **Obwohl** *es hilfreich ist, ein wenig Deutsch zu sprechen, sprechen viele Deutsche auch ziemlich gutes Englisch, besonders in touristischen Gebieten.* **Trotzdem** *rate ich dir, ein paar Grundlagen zu lernen. Das wird überall sehr begrüßt!*

Gina: *Das werde ich* **tun, weil** *ich mich immer gerne in die Kultur integriere. Gibt es sonst noch Tipps, die du mir geben kannst?*

Wilhelm: *Ja,* **wenn** *es regnet, was in Deutschland manchmal der Fall ist, gibt es viele Museen und Indoor-Aktivitäten. Und* **weil** *du Essen ja so liebst, probiere auf jeden Fall einen Schweinebraten – der ist in Deutschland besonders gut!*

Gina: *Ich werde alle diese Tipps beachten. Danke, Wilhelm!*

Wilhelm: *Gern geschehen und gute Reise, Gina!*

DEUTSCHLANDS JUWELEN (GERMANY'S HIDDEN GEMS)

Rüdiger and Katrin sit in a cozy café and talk about their travels through Germany.

Rüdiger: Katrin, **obwohl** ich schon viele Städte in Deutschland besucht habe, finde ich, dass Heidelberg einzigartig ist.

Katrin: Das stimmt, Rüdiger. Heidelberg ist wunderschön, **vor allem** wegen des Schlosses und des Neckars. **Trotzdem** hat Dresden auch seinen besonderen Charme mit der Frauenkirche und der Elbe.

Rüdiger: Das kann ich nicht abstreiten. Dresden ist wirklich beeindruckend. Aber was hältst du von München? Viele sagen, es sei die schönste Stadt Deutschlands, **weil** sie eine perfekte Mischung aus Moderne und Tradition bietet.

Katrin: Ja, München ist auch atemberaubend. Aber mir gefällt Hamburg besser, **denn** es hat diesen maritimen Charakter, der so einladend ist. **Obwohl** es oft regnet, gibt es dort so viel zu sehen und zu tun.

Rüdiger: **Wenn** man von Regen spricht, denke ich an Köln. **Obwohl** es manchmal grau ist, strahlt die Stadt immer. **Wenn** ich noch mal die Gelegenheit bekäme, **würde** ich sofort wieder dorthin reisen.

Katrin: Das verstehe ich vollkommen. Und **wenn** du jemals wieder hinfährst, lass es mich wissen. **Vielleicht könnten** wir zusammen reisen und die Kölner Spezialitäten genießen.

Rüdiger: Das klingt nach einem guten Plan! Aber **trotzdem** müssen wir uns auch Städte wie Berlin und Frankfurt ansehen. Jede Stadt hat etwas Einzigartiges zu bieten, **denn** Deutschland ist so vielfältig.

Katrin: Absolut! Es gibt immer etwas Neues zu entdecken, **egal wo** man ist.

2.1 DIE VERWENDUNG VON „OBWOHL" UND „TROTZDEM"
(USAGE OF „OBWOHL" AND „TROTZDEM")

„Obwohl" and „trotzdem" are two vital connectors that express contrast or contradiction. While both can be used to indicate that something happens in spite of something else, they are used in different syntactic structures.

„obwohl"

↳ „Obwohl" is a subordinating conjunction that introduces a subordinate clause. It can be translated to "although" or "even though" in English. The verb in the clause introduced by „obwohl" moves to the end.

Structure with „obwohl"
Main Clause + obwohl + Subject + ..., Verb

Sie geht joggen, obwohl es regnet.
(She goes jogging even though it's raining.)

„trotzdem"

↳ „Trotzdem" is an adverb and can be translated to "nevertheless" or "still" in English. It is generally placed at the beginning or in the middle of the main clause to indicate a contrast to the previous statement.

Structure with „trotzdem"
Main Clause + trotzdem + Rest of the Sentence

Es regnet und trotzdem geht sie joggen.
(It's raining and still she goes jogging.)

While both „obwohl" and „trotzdem" can exist in simple contrasting sentences, they're often used in more complex structures to provide depth, nuance, and detail:

Er hat wenig geschlafen, obwohl er weiß, dass er morgen einen wichtigen Termin hat.
Trotzdem fühlt er sich fit und ausgeruht.
(He slept little, even though he knows he has an important appointment tomorrow. Nevertheless, he feels fit and rested.)

In this example, „obwohl" and „trotzdem" work together to build a narrative of contradiction, expressing a scenario where, against all expectations, the individual feels rested despite minimal sleep. This showcases the richness these connectors can bring to expressing nuanced scenarios in the German language.

> **ⓘ GUT ZU WISSEN**
>
> Don't leave Germany without trying a traditional *Bratwurst* or *Sauerbraten*. In Austria, indulge in a slice of *Sachertorte* or some *Apfelstrudel*. And in Switzerland, savor the world-renowned Swiss chocolate and fondue. Each region has its own specialties, so ask locals for their recommendations!

2.2 KONDITIONALSÄTZE
(CONDITIONAL SENTENCES)

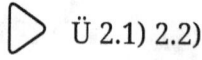 Ü 2.1) 2.2)

Conditional sentences, commonly referred to as 'if' clauses, are a crucial component of German grammar. These sentences consist of a main clause and a conditional (or subordinate) clause. The primary role of these structures is to depict actions or events and their possible results, based on certain conditions or hypothetical situations. By using them, you're essentially conveying the idea of "If this happens (or happened), then that will (or would) happen."

There are three primary types of conditional sentences in German, and they differ based on their likelihood or time reference.

Typ 1: **Real Conditions**

→ Real Conditions express a probable or possible situation in the present or future, as well as its likely result or consequence. This type is mostly concerned with real and likely scenarios, situations that could genuinely happen given a specific condition.

Structure of *Typ 1*	
Main clause	Present Tense or Future Tense
Subordinate clause	wenn + Present Tense

Examples:

Wenn du Hunger hast, gibt es Kuchen in der Küche.
(If you are hungry, there is cake in the kitchen.)

Wenn es morgen sonnig ist, gehe ich schwimmen.
(If it's sunny tomorrow, I'll go swimming.)

Wenn du das Fenster öffnest, kommt frische Luft herein.
(If you open the window, fresh air will come in.)

Typ 2: **Unreal Conditions in the Present**

→ This type addresses hypothetical situations that are contrary to the current reality. They depict an unreal or improbable situation in the present or future and its hypothetical outcome.

Structure of *Typ 2*	
Main clause	Konjunktiv II or Würde-Form
Subordinate clause	wenn + Konjunktiv II

Examples:

Ich würde ein Schloss kaufen, wenn ich Millionär wäre.
(I would buy a castle if I were a millionaire.)

Wenn du fliegen könntest, wohin würdest du reisen?
(If you could fly, where would you go?)

Er würde uns besuchen, wenn er Zeit hätte.
(He would visit us if he had the time.)

Typ 3: **Unreal Conditions in the Past**

↳ *Typ 3* focuses on hypothetical situations in the past. These are actions or situations that didn't happen but are being reflected upon regarding what might have occurred if things had been different.

Structure of *Typ 3*	
Main clause	Konjunktiv II of „haben" or „sein" + Past Participle
Subordinate clause	wenn + Plusquamperfekt

Examples:

Ich hätte anders gehandelt, wenn ich das gewusst hätte.
(I would have acted differently if I had known that.)

Sie hätte die Prüfung bestanden, wenn sie das Buch gelesen hätte.
(She would have passed the exam if she had read the book.)

Wir hätten den Film nicht verpasst, wenn wir früher angekommen wären.
(We wouldn't have missed the movie if we had arrived earlier.)

One can start a sentence with the „wenn"-clause to emphasize the condition, although the main clause can also precede the „wenn"-clause:

<u>Wenn</u> ich Zeit habe, werde ich das Buch lesen. (If I have time, I will read the book.)

Ich werde das Buch lesen, <u>wenn</u> ich Zeit habe. (I will read the book if I have time.)

In clauses beginning with „wenn", the <u>verb</u> is pushed to the end. This holds true for all three types of conditionals. In the main clause of conditional sentences, the verb (or „<u>würde</u>") usually occupies the second position:

Wenn du helfen <u>könntest</u>, wäre ich sehr dankbar.
(If you could help, I would be very grateful.)

Ich <u>wäre</u> sehr dankbar, wenn du mir helfen könntest.
(I would be very grateful if you could help me.)

While „wenn" is the primary word for "if" in German, there are other words like „<u>falls</u>" (in case) that can be used in certain contexts.

<u>Falls</u> du morgen Zeit hast, können wir ins Kino gehen.
(In case you have time tomorrow, we can go to the cinema.)

2.3 DIE VERWENDUNG VON „DENN" UND „WEIL" (USING „DENN" AND „WEIL")

Both „denn" and „weil" are subordinating conjunctions used to express cause or reason. They are crucial for constructing causal relationships between clauses. However, they function differently in terms of sentence structure.

„weil" (because)

↳ When „weil" is used, it introduces a dependent clause, which means the main verb will be placed at the end of the clause.

Structure
<u>Subject</u> + <u>Verb</u> + ..., <u>weil</u> + <u>Subject</u> + ... + <u>Verb</u>

<u>Ich</u> <u>gehe</u> ins Kino, <u>weil</u> <u>ich</u> den Film <u>sehen</u> möchte.
(I'm going to the cinema because I want to see the movie.)

„denn" (because/for)

↳ On the other hand, „denn" introduces an independent clause, meaning the word order remains the same as in a main clause, with the verb following the subject.

Structure
Subject + Verb + ..., *denn* Subject + Verb + ...

Ich gehe ins Kino, denn ich mag den Schauspieler.
(I'm going to the cinema because I like the actor.)

Transportmittel (Means of Transport)	
(das) Auto	car
(der) Bus	bus
(die) Bahn	train/railway
(das) Fahrrad	bicycle
fahren	(to) drive/ride
(das) Flugzeug	airplane
(das) Schiff	ship
(der) Roller	scooter
fliegen	(to) fly
(die) U-Bahn	subway/underground
(die) Straßenbahn	tram/streetcar
gehen	(to) walk
(das) Taxi	taxi
(das) Motorrad	motorcycle
radeln	(to) cycle
(das) Boot	boat
(die) Fähre	ferry

Reiseempfehlungen für Deutschland (Travel Recommendations for Germany) – *Wortschatz* (Vocabulary)

(das) Reiseziel (-e) [n.]	destination
entscheiden [v.]	(to) decide
sicher [adj.]	for sure
anfangen [v.]	(to) begin
historisch [adj.]	historical
(die) Stadt (Städte) [n.]	city
(das) Essen (-) [n.]	food
möglich [adj.]	possible
(das) Highlight (-s) [n.]	highlight
unbedingt [adv.]	absolutely
besuchen [v.]	(to) visit
(die) Vielfalt (-) [n.]	variety
regional [adj.]	regional
fantastisch [adj.]	fantastic
(das) Zugsystem (-e) [n.]	train system
zuverlässig [adj.]	reliable
(die) Sprachbarriere (-n) [n.]	language barrier
fließend [adj.]	fluent
wohl [adj.]	well
hilfreich [adj.]	helpful
besonders [adv.]	special
touristisch [adj.]	touristy
(das) Gebiet (-e) [n.]	area
(die) Grundlage (-n) [n.]	base
schätzen [v.]	(to) appreciate
(der) Tipp (-s) [n.]	tip
regnen [v.]	(to) rain
(das) Museum (Museen) [n.]	museum
beachten [v.]	(to) note

Deutschlands Juwelen (Germany's Hidden Gems) – Wortschatz (Vocabulary)

obwohl [conj.]	although
einzigartig [adj.]	unique
wunderschön [adj.]	beautiful
(das) Schloss (Schlösser) [n.]	castle
abstreiten [v.]	(to) deny
beeindruckend [adj.]	impressive
(der) Charme (-) [n.]	charm
(die) Mischung (-en) [n.]	mixture
modern [adj.]	modern
bieten [v.]	(to) offer
atemberaubend [adj.]	stunning
maritim [adj.]	maritime
(der) Charakter (-) [n.]	character
grau [adj.]	gray
strahlen [v.]	(to) radiate
sofort [adv.]	instant
vollkommen [adv.]	perfect
hingehen [v.]	(to) go there
(die) Spezialität (-en) [n.]	specialty
ansehen [v.]	(to) look at
vielfältig [adj.]	diverse
entdecken [v.]	(to) discover

Section 3

UNVERGESSLICHE REISEERLEBNISSE TEILEN
(SHARING MEMORABLE TRAVEL TALES)

 KULINARISCHE ABENTEUER IN DEUTSCHLAND
(CULINARY ADVENTURES IN GERMANY)

Veronika, a food blogger, is chatting with her friend Thorsten about her recent culinary journey through various cities in Germany.

Veronika: Thorsten! Du glaubst nicht, was ich **während** meiner Reise durch Deutschland alles probiert habe!

Thorsten: Ah, Veronika! Erzähl mir alles! Wie war's in Berlin?

Veronika: Berlin war unglaublich! **Um Punkt Mitternacht** habe ich Currywurst direkt unter dem Fernsehturm gegessen. Echt ein Erlebnis!

Thorsten: Das klingt, als ob du auf Wolke sieben schwebst. Und wie war München?

Veronika: Oh, München! **Während** des Mittagessens in einem Biergarten habe ich die beste Weißwurst meines Lebens gehabt. Und dazu ein frisch gezapftes Bier — es war **um die Mittagszeit**, und die Sonne schien so schön.

Thorsten: Das klingt nach einem echten Schlemmerparadies. Da läuft mir glatt das Wasser im Mund zusammen!

Veronika: Das war es definitiv! Und warte, bis du von Köln hörst. **Um genau sechs Uhr** abends habe ich mich in einem kleinen Café niedergelassen und den berühmten Kölner Senf probiert.

Thorsten: Echt jetzt? **Während** der Hauptverkehrszeit in einem Café sitzen und Senf probieren? Das ist wirklich ein kulinarisches Abenteuer!

Veronika: Ja, und das ist nur die Spitze des Eisbergs! Es gibt so viele kulinarische Juwelen zu entdecken.

Thorsten: Du hast echt ein tolles Leben! Sich **während** des ganzen Tages nur ums Essen zu kümmern, das wäre auch was für mich!

PÜNKTLICH WIE DIE DEUTSCHE BAHN
(PUNCTUAL LIKE THE GERMAN RAILWAY)

*Die Deutsche Bahn – ein Symbol für Pünktlichkeit? Nun, in einem Paralleluniversum vielleicht! **Während** sich viele Deutsche über einen verpassten Bus ärgern würden, sehen sie es mittlerweile als nationales Hobby an, auf verspätete Züge zu warten. Es ist **fast** eine Tradition, **pünktlich um 7 Uhr** am Bahnsteig zu stehen und festzustellen, dass der Zug ... nun ja, sagen wir mal, eine kleine kreative Pause einlegt.*

***Zeit ist Geld** — aber in Deutschland könnte man auch sagen: „Zeit ist die Gelegenheit, ein neues Buch zu beginnen, **während** man auf den Zug wartet." Und wenn der Zug dann endlich einfährt? Dann kann man sich zurücklehnen und die Landschaft genießen — **während** man hofft, dass man **um 12 Uhr** (anstatt 10 Uhr) noch rechtzeitig zum Ziel kommt.*

*Das Sprichwort „**Alle Wege führen nach Rom**" bekommt in Deutschland eine neue Wendung: „**Alle Gleise führen zu ... einem weiteren verspäteten Zug**". Aber sehen wir es positiv: Dank der Deutschen Bahn lernt man Geduld, findet neue Freunde am Bahnsteig und hat immer eine gute Ausrede, warum man zu spät kommt!*

Zum Abschluss: Ja, die Deutsche Bahn hat ihre Tücken, aber ohne sie wäre das Leben der Deutschen doch ein ganzes Stück weniger unterhaltsam!

3.1 DIE UHRZEIT (THE TIME)   Ü 3.1)

Time-telling is a fundamental skill in any language. In German, like in many languages, there are specific patterns and rules to express the time of day. Here we will explore the nuances of telling the time in German.

In German, when telling the time, one commonly uses the verb <u>sein</u> (to be).

Es <u>ist</u> ein Uhr. (It is one o'clock.)

Formal vs. Informal Time-telling:

Formal Time:	This is the 24-hour clock system, commonly used in official scenarios, like on train schedules or in business meetings.
Informal Time:	A 12-hour clock system, more common in daily conversations among friends and family.

English Time	Formal German (24-hour format)	Written Out Version	Informal German	Notes
1:00	01:00 Uhr	ein Uhr	ein Uhr	„Uhr" can be seen as equivalent to "o'clock" in English.
2:15	02:15 Uhr	zwei Uhr fünfzehn	Viertel nach zwei	„Viertel nach" means "a quarter past".
2:30	02:30 Uhr	zwei Uhr dreißig	halb drei	„halb" indicates half an hour before the upcoming hour.
2:45	02:45 Uhr	zwei Uhr fünfundvierzig	Viertel vor drei	„Viertel vor" means "a quarter to".
15:00	15:00 Uhr	fünfzehn Uhr	drei Uhr (nachmittags)	„nachmittags" denotes afternoon time.

Asking and Giving Time:

To ask for the time in German, you can say:

Wie spät ist es?   *Wie viel Uhr ist es?*
(What time is it?)   (How much clock is it? – *direct translation*)

Responses can be structured as:

Es ist [time].

Parts of the Day:

When discussing time, Germans often mention the part of the day to provide context, especially in informal settings.

morgens	→	during the morning	→	(e.g., 5:00 to 9:00)
vormittags	→	late morning	→	(e.g., 9:00 to 12:00)
mittags	→	noon and early afternoon	→	(e.g., 12:00 to 14:00)
nachmittags	→	during the afternoon	→	(e.g., 14:00 to 18:00)
abends	→	during the evening	→	(e.g., 18:00 to 22:00)
nachts	→	during the night	→	(e.g., 22:00 to 5:00)

Minutes, Quarters, and Half Hours:

In German, apart from stating exact minutes, the quarters and half-hour indications are commonly used.

- *nach* → past (e.g., zehn nach drei – ten past three)
- *vor* → to (e.g., zehn vor drei – ten to three)

- *Viertel*
  - ↳ Viertel nach [hour] → a quarter past [hour]
  - ↳ Viertel vor [hour] → a quarter to [hour]

- *halb* [hour] → half to the next hour

Note: The use of „halb" is a common point of confusion. In German, „halb drei" means 2:30, not 3:30 as a direct translation might suggest.

3.2 REDEWENDUNGEN UND IDIOME (IDIOMS AND PHRASES)  Ü 3.2)

„Kleinvieh macht auch Mist"

(lit. small livestock also make poop)

Idioms and phrases enrich a language, adding layers of meaning, cultural references, and humor. They are phrases or expressions whose meanings aren't deducible from the literal definitions and arrangement of the words themselves. While they can be challenging to learn for non-native speakers due to their figurative nature, they're vital for gaining fluency and understanding the cultural nuances of the German-speaking world.

Idioms provide insights into a culture's history, values, and ways of thinking. For instance, the German idiom „Das ist nicht mein Bier" translates literally to "That's not my beer", but it means "That's none of my business". This expression might hint at the significance of beer in German culture, where communal beer drinking is a traditional social activity.

Tips for Learning Idioms:

- Context is King: Always learn idioms in context. This helps in understanding the situation in which it is most appropriately used.

- Group Similar Idioms: Some idioms have themes, like those related to animals, body parts, or nature. Group these idioms together to make them easier to learn and remember.

- Visualize the Literal Meaning: This can be a fun way to remember the idiom. For instance, picturing someone with „Tomaten auf den Augen" (tomatoes on the eyes) can be an amusing way to remember the phrase means being oblivious to something obvious.

German Idiom	Literal Translation	English Equivalent
Mit jemandem ein Hühnchen rupfen	To pluck a chicken with someone	To have a bone to pick with someone
Das ist ein Katzensprung	That's a cat's jump	It's a stone's throw away
Jemandem einen Bären aufbinden	To tie a bear onto someone	To pull someone's leg/ to deceive someone
Auf Wolke sieben sein	To be on cloud seven	To be on cloud nine (to be extremely happy)
Den Nagel auf den Kopf treffen	To hit the nail on the head	To hit the nail on the head
Nicht alle Tassen im Schrank haben	Not to have all cups in the cupboard	Not to have all one's marbles (to be a bit crazy)
Schwein haben	To have a pig	To be a lucky dog or lucky duck
Das fünfte Rad am Wagen sein	To be the fifth wheel on the car	To be the third wheel (to be superfluous)
Um den heißen Brei herumreden	To talk around the hot porridge	To beat around the bush
Ins Gras beißen	To bite into the grass	To bite the dust (to die or fail)
Da liegt der Hund begraben	That's where the dog is buried	That's the crux of the matter
Das Leben ist kein Ponyhof	Life isn't a pony farm	Life isn't all fun and games
Durch die Blume sagen	To say something through the flower	To sugarcoat the pill

Notfallsituationen (Emergency Situations)	
(der) Notfall	emergency
(die) Hilfe	help
(die) Polizei	police
(der) Krankenwagen	ambulance
(das) Krankenhaus	hospital
(die) Verletzung	injury
(der) Unfall	accident
(die) Feuerwehr	fire brigade/fire department
(die) Gefahr	danger
(der) Arzt	doctor
(die) Apotheke	pharmacy
(das) Medikament	medication
(die) Erste Hilfe	first aid
(der) Notruf	emergency call
(die) Sicherheit	safety

Kulinarische Abenteuer in Deutschland (Culinary Adventures in Germany) – Wortschatz (Vocabulary)

probieren [v.]	(to) taste, try
unglaublich [adj.]	incredible
direkt [adv.]	direct
(der) Fernsehturm (Fernsehtürme) [n.]	television tower
(das) Erlebnis (-se) [n.]	experience
schweben [v.]	(to) float
(die) Wolke (-n) [n.]	cloud
(das) Mittagessen (-) [n.]	lunch
(der) Biergarten (Biergärten) [n.]	beer garden
frisch [adj.]	fresh
zapfen [v.]	(to) tap
(das) Schlemmerparadies (-e) [n.]	feasting paradise
sich niederlassen [v.]	(to) settle down
berühmt [adj.]	famous
probieren [v.]	(to) taste
(die) Hauptverkehrszeit (-en) [n.]	rush hour
(der) Senf (-e) [n.]	mustard
(der) Eisberg (-e) [n.]	iceberg
kümmern [v.]	(to) take care of

Im Takt der Gleise (In the Rhythm of the Rails) – Wortschatz (Vocabulary)

(das) Symbol (-e) [n.]	symbol
pünktlich [adj.]	on time
zumindest [adv.]	at least
endlich [adv.]	finally
sich zurücklehnen [v.]	(to) recline
(die) Landschaft (-en) [n.]	landscape
genießen [v.]	(to) enjoy
rechtzeitig [adj.]	in time
(das) Ziel (-e) [n.]	destination
anstatt [prep.]	instead of
(die) Ausrede (-n) [n.]	excuse
hell [adj.]	bright
verspätet [adj.]	belated
(die) Wendung (-en) [n.]	turn
(das) Sprichwort (Sprichwörter) [n.]	proverb
(der) Bahnsteig (-e) [n.]	platform
(die) Geduld (-) [n.]	patience
(die) Tücke (-n) [n.]	perfidy
unterhaltsam [adj.]	entertaining

ÜBUNGEN (EXERCISES)

Ü 1.1) Zu jedem Bild wird eine Beschreibung gegeben. Deine Aufgabe ist es, die richtige Getrennt- oder Zusammenschreibung für das hervorgehobene Wortpaar zu wählen.

A description is given for each picture. Your task is to choose the correct hyphenation or contraction for the highlighted word pair.

Example:
Die Sonne |geht| |unter|.
untergehen

a.
Er |klopft| |an| die Tür.

b.
Sie |bindet| den Schal |um|.

c.
Der Junge |greift| |zu|.

d.
Der Mann |wartet| |ab|.

e.
Sie |hängt| die Uhr |auf|.

Ü 1.2) Entscheide, ob die folgenden Worte getrennt oder zusammengeschrieben werden. Korrigiere sie gegebenenfalls.

Decide whether the following phrases should be written separately or compounded. Correct them if necessary.

Example:

☒		☒	
zuhause	*oder*	*zu Hause?*	*Both options are correct.*

☐ wiedersehen oder ☐ wieder sehen | ☐ gutmachen oder ☐ gut machen

☐ stattfinden oder ☐ statt finden | ☐ festhalten oder ☐ fest halten

☐ radfahren oder ☐ Rad fahren | ☐ liegenbleiben oder ☐ liegen bleiben

☐ teilnehmen oder ☐ teil nehmen | ☐ kennenlernen oder ☐ kennen lernen

Ü 2.1) Ergänze die folgenden Sätze, um vollständige Konditionalsätze zu bilden.

Complete the following sentences to form full conditional sentences.

Example: Wenn es regnet, _____ (ich / nehmen) einen Schirm.
↓
Wenn es regnet, **nehme ich** einen Schirm.

a. Wenn du _____ (kommen / früh), bekommst du einen guten Platz.

b. Ich würde ihm helfen, wenn ich _____ (können).

c. Sie _____ (sein / traurig), wenn ihr Hund wegliefe.

d. Er würde ins Kino gehen, wenn er Geld _____ (haben).

e. Wenn es morgen _____ (regnen), bleibt sie zu Hause.

f. Du würdest besser schlafen, wenn du weniger _____ (fernsehen).

g. Wenn sie rechtzeitig _____ (abfahren), erreicht sie das Ziel pünktlich.

h. Ich würde dir das Buch leihen, wenn ich es _____ (nicht / verlieren / haben).

i. Wenn sie weiter so _____ (arbeiten / hart), wird sie bald befördert.

j. Er _____ (sein / froh), wenn du ihm hilfst.

Ü 2.1) Stelle dir vor, du lebst für einen Tag in einer Parallelwelt, in der alles anders ist. Beantworte die Fragen, indem du vollständige Konditionalsätze bildest.
Imagine that for one day you live in a parallel universe where everything is different. Answer the questions by forming complete conditional sentences.

Example:

Question: *Was würdest du tun, wenn Hunde sprechen könnten?*
Answer: *Wenn Hunde sprechen könnten, würde ich stundenlang mit meinem Hund plaudern.*

a. Question: Was würdest du machen, wenn Wasser plötzlich nach Schokolade schmecken würde?

  Answer: _____

b. Question: Wie würdest du deinen Tag verbringen, wenn jede Stunde 120 Minuten hätte?

  Answer: _____

c. Question: Was würdest du tun, wenn Tiere dich um Rat fragen könnten?

  Answer: _____

d. Question: Was würdest du machen, wenn du durch Gedankenkraft Gegenstände bewegen könntest?

  Answer: _____

e. Question: Wie würdest du dich verhalten, wenn jeder gelogene Satz sofort sichtbar auf deiner Stirn erscheinen würde?

  Answer: _____

Ü 3.1) Schau dir die Bilder von Uhren an und schreibe die Uhrzeit, die sie anzeigen, in Worten auf.

Look at the pictures of the clocks and write the time in words.

Example:

a.   b.   c.

Es ist...   Es ist...   Es ist...   Es ist...

Viertel nach sieben.   _____   _____   _____

                         _____   _____   _____

d.   e.   f.   g.

Es ist...   Es ist...   Es ist...   Es ist...

_____   _____   _____   _____

_____   _____   _____   _____

Ü 3.2) Ergänze die fehlenden Wörter in den folgenden deutschen Redewendungen und Idiomen. Dann versuche, deren Bedeutung in eigenen Worten zu beschreiben oder übersetze sie ins Englische.

Fill in the missing words in the following German idioms and phrases. Then try to describe their meaning in your own words or translate them into English.

Example: *Jemandem einen Bären _____.* → *Jemandem einen Bären aufbinden.*

→ *Jemandem etwas Unwahres erzählen / Telling someone something untrue.*

a. Das ist nicht mein _____.

b. Er hat Tomaten auf den _____.

c. Sie hat Schmetterlinge im _____.

d. Um den heißen Brei _____.

e. Das ist ein Tropfen auf den _____.

f. Jemandem auf den _____ treten.

Unit 5

BILDUNG UND KARRIERE

(EDUCATION AND CAREER)

Unit V, titled *„Bildung und Karriere"*, focuses on the application of the German language in educational and professional settings. The unit begins with *„In der deutschen Arbeitswelt gedeihen"*, where you'll explore language used in the workplace, learning about formal structures and vocabulary relevant to professional environments. This includes understanding purpose and cause clauses, the art of nominalizing verbs, and the appropriate use of interjections in a work context. The next section, „Fort- und Weiterbildung", explores language skills essential for professional development and continuous learning, including constructions like „um ... zu" and detailed exploration of infinitive clauses. The unit concludes with *„Das Bildungssystem in Deutschland erkunden"*, providing insights into the German educational system. Here, you'll learn about compound nouns and N-declension, crucial for discussing academic subjects and navigating educational conversations. This unit aims to equip you with the language skills necessary for success in academic and professional pursuits in the German-speaking world.

Section 1

IN DER DEUTSCHEN ARBEITSWELT ERFOLGREICH SEIN
(THRIVING IN THE GERMAN WORKPLACE)

 ARBEITEN IN DEUTSCHLAND: KULTURELLE UNTERSCHIEDE UND HERAUSFORDERUNGEN
(WORKING IN GERMANY: CULTURAL DIFFERENCES AND CHALLENGES)

Fiona, a British expat, is having coffee with her German colleague, Konstantin, discussing her experiences and challenges working in Germany.

Fiona: Konstantin, ich muss zugeben, das Arbeiten hier ist anders als in England. Um mich besser integrieren zu können, würde ich gerne die Unterschiede besser verstehen.

Konstantin: Oh, **tatsächlich**? Inwiefern findest du es denn anders?

Fiona: Nun, zum einen sind hier alle sehr pünktlich. In England, wenn ein Meeting um 10 Uhr beginnt, wäre es okay, ein paar Minuten später zu erscheinen. Aber **hier**, wenn es 10 Uhr heißt, dann meint man auch 10 Uhr!

Konstantin: Ach, das! **Ja**, Pünktlichkeit ist in Deutschland eine Art von Höflichkeit. Es zeigt Respekt für die Zeit der anderen.

Fiona: Das ergibt Sinn. Außerdem habe ich bemerkt, dass die **Kommunikation** sehr direkt ist. Nicht, dass das schlecht wäre, aber es war zu Beginn eine echte **Umstellung** für mich.

Konstantin: Verstehe. **Na ja**, das liegt daran, dass wir Wert auf **Klarheit** legen. Statt lange um den heißen Brei herumzureden, kommen wir direkt zur Sache. Das kann am Anfang überwältigend sein, hat aber den **Vorteil**, dass Missverständnisse vermieden werden.

Fiona: Das sehe ich ein. Und ich schätze auch die **Effizienz**, mit der hier gearbeitet wird. Es scheint, als ob jeder genau wüsste, was sein **Ziel** ist und warum er es tut.

Konstantin: Das ist oft der Fall. **Hm**, noch einen Kaffee?

Fiona: Oh, **ja bitte**! Und danke, Konstantin. Dieses Gespräch hat mir wirklich geholfen, einige Dinge aus einer neuen Perspektive zu sehen.

Konstantin: **Gern geschehen**! Immer gut, über solche Dinge zu sprechen. Es hilft, Brücken zu bauen.

WORK-LIFE-BALANCE IN DEUTSCHLAND: EIN SCHLÜSSEL ZUM GLÜCK
(WORK-LIFE BALANCE IN GERMANY: A KEY TO HAPPINESS)

Ach, Work-Life-Balance! In Deutschland hat das Streben nach einem Gleichgewicht zwischen Arbeit und Freizeit in den letzten Jahren erheblich an Bedeutung gewonnen. **Warum?** *Die Antwort liegt in der Erkenntnis, dass Zufriedenheit und Wohlbefinden nicht nur durch beruflichen Erfolg definiert werden.*

Daher *haben viele Unternehmen damit begonnen, flexiblere Arbeitszeiten* **anzubieten***, um die* **Zufriedenheit** *ihrer Mitarbeiter zu erhöhen. Dies dient* **nicht nur** *dem Zweck, das Wohlbefinden zu fördern, sondern hat auch den* **Vorteil***, die Produktivität zu steigern. Denn wenn Mitarbeiter zufrieden sind, führt dies oft zu besseren Arbeitsergebnissen.*

Zudem *hat die* **Förderung** *von Freizeitaktivitäten einen hohen Stellenwert. Sei es das* **Lesen** *eines Buches, der Besuch eines Fitnessstudios oder das* **Genießen** *eines Hobbys — all dies trägt dazu bei, den Geist zu erfrischen und den täglichen Stress abzubauen.* **Oh***, welche Freude es doch bringt, wenn man die richtige Balance findet!*

1.1 FINAL- UND KAUSALSÄTZE (PURPOSE AND CAUSE CLAUSES) ▷ Ü 1.1)

Finalsätze **(Purpose Clauses)** express an intention or a goal behind an action. Imagine you're setting out on a journey. While the journey itself is essential, the destination or the reason for the journey adds depth and context. In language terms, you might be learning German — but why? Is it to study at a university, to connect with family roots, or to enjoy German literature in its original form? This "why" or purpose is expressed through *Finalsätze*.

A frequently used conjunction for purpose clauses is „*damit*". The conjunction „*damit*" can be directly translated to "so that" in English. Another formulation employed is „*um ... zu*", which translates to "in order to". The distinction between these two is subtle but significant:

damit: Generally preferred when the subjects in the main and subordinate clauses differ.

> ↳ *Er lernt Deutsch, <u>damit</u> er in Berlin arbeiten kann.*
> (He is learning German so that he can work in Berlin.)

um ... zu: Used when the subject in both clauses remains unchanged.

> ↳ *Sie spart Geld, <u>um</u> sich ein neues Auto <u>zu</u> kaufen.*
> (She is saving in order to buy herself a new car.)

Kausalsätze (cause clauses), on the other hand, explain the reason behind an action. If purpose clauses are the destinations of our linguistic journey, cause clauses are the starting points. They provide the background, the foundation on which actions are built.

For cause clauses, the conjunctions of choice are „weil", „da", and „denn". Each has its own nuanced usage:

weil: A commonly used conjunction in spoken German. It places the verb at the end of the clause.

↳ *Er kommt nicht zur Party, weil er krank ist.*
(He isn't coming to the party because he is sick.)

da: While it's synonymous with „weil" „da" is more prevalent in written German or when emphasizing the cause.

↳ *Sie ist glücklich, da sie die Prüfung bestanden hat.*
(She is happy since she passed the exam.)

denn: This conjunction maintains the verb's position and is versatile in its use.

„*Wir bleiben heute zu Hause, denn es ist zu kalt draußen.*"
(We're staying at home today, for it's too cold outside.)

To grasp these clauses, it's imperative to view them not merely as grammatical structures but as windows into the German thought process. The German language places significant emphasis on the logic, intention, and causality of actions. Whether you're explaining a reason or elaborating on a purpose, these clauses provide clarity, offering listeners or readers insight into the deeper motivations behind actions.

1.2 NOMINALISIERUNG VON VERBEN (NOMINALIZATION OF VERBS)   ▷ Ü 1.2), 1.3)

In German, one of the fascinating linguistic features is the ability to transform verbs into nouns through a process known as *Nominalisierung von Verben*. This transformation, while offering linguistic versatility, embeds layers of meaning into sentences, allowing for richer and more nuanced communication.

At its core, nominalization captures the essence of a verb and packages it as a more abstract, generic noun. This subtle shift in representation, while maintaining the verb's essential action, allows for a unique kind of expressiveness. These newly minted nouns adopt the neuter gender and capitalize on the verb's infinitive form. For instance, *schreiben* (to write) becomes *das Schreiben* (writing) and *lesen* (to read) evolves into *das Lesen* (reading).

Examples	
lesen (to read) - *das Lesen*	**schreiben (to write) - *das Schreiben***
Lesen macht Spaß. (Reading is fun.) *Das Lesen eines guten Buches ist entspannend.* (Reading a good book is relaxing.)	*Schreiben ist eine Kunst.* (Writing is an art.) *Das Schreiben eines Romans dauert oft Jahre.* (Writing a novel often takes years.)
spielen (to play) - *das Spielen*	**kochen (to cook) - *das Kochen***
Spielen hält jung. (Playing keeps [one] young.) *Das Spielen eines Instruments erfordert Übung.* (Playing an instrument requires practice.)	*Kochen ist Therapie für mich.* (Cooking is therapy for me.) *Das Kochen kann manchmal stundenlang dauern.* (Cooking can sometimes take hours.)
reisen (to travel) - *das Reisen*	**lernen (to learn) - *das Lernen***
Reisen erweitert den Horizont. (Travel broadens the horizon.) *Das Reisen in ferne Länder ist lehrreich.* (Traveling to distant countries is educational.)	*Wir hören nie auf zu lernen.* (We never stop learning.) *Das Lernen einer neuen Sprache ist herausfordernd.* (Learning a new language is challenging.)

While the process of nominalizing verbs might seem straightforward, there are subtleties to keep in mind.

- **Cases and Prepositions:** These nominalized verbs can take on cases and be governed by prepositions, just like any other noun. For instance, „*mit dem Schreiben beginnen*" (to begin with writing) and „*am Lesen sein*" (to be reading).

- **Compound Nouns:** One of the fascinating aspects of German nominalization is its ability to create compound nouns. Consider the word „*staubsaugen*" (to vacuum). Its nominalized form, „*das Staubsaugen*", translates to "the act of vacuuming". Another example is „*Auto fahren*" (to drive a car) becoming „*das Autofahren*" (the act of driving).

- **Adjective Usage:** Since these nominalized verbs behave like nouns, they can be modified by adjectives, just like any other noun. „*Das schnelle Lesen*" (fast reading) or „*das methodische Lernen*" (methodical learning) are some examples of this usage.

1.3 INTERJEKTIONEN (INTERJECTIONS) ▷ Ü 1.4)

Interjections are short words or phrases used to express strong emotion, surprise, or to capture the listener's attention. They can stand alone or be inserted into a sentence, and they often don't have a grammatical connection to other parts of the sentence.

Interjections can express a wide range of emotions such as happiness, surprise, anger, or sadness:

Hurra! (Hooray!) *Oh!* (Oh!) *Autsch!* (Ouch!)

They can also be used to capture attention or to greet someone:

Hallo! (Hello!) *He!* or *Hey!* (Hey!)

Interjections are commonly used as responses to express how someone feels about something quickly and without a full sentence:

Ja! (Yes!) *Nein!* (No!)

Interjection	Usage	English Equivalent	Example Sentence	Translation
Oh	Expressing surprise	Oh	**Oh**, das habe ich nicht gewusst!	Oh, I didn't know that!
Autsch	Expressing pain	Ouch	**Autsch**, das tut weh!	Ouch, that hurts!
Hurra	Expressing joy or celebration	Hooray	**Hurra**, wir haben gewonnen!	Hooray, we won!
Hm	Thinking, pondering	Hmm	**Hm**, das ist eine gute Frage.	Hmm, that's a good question.
Eh	Expressing doubt or confusion	Huh	**Eh**, was meinst du?	Huh, what do you mean?
Uff	Expressing relief or tiredness	Phew	**Uff**, das war knapp!	Phew, that was close!
Igitt	Expressing disgust	Yuck	**Igitt**, das schmeckt ja furchtbar!	Yuck, that tastes awful!
Na	Greeting or to initiate conversation	Well	**Na**, wie geht's dir?	Well, how are you?
He	To get someone's attention	Hey	**He**, kannst du mir helfen?	Hey, can you help me?
Psst	Asking for silence or to be quiet	Shush	**Psst**, ich kann nichts hören!	Shush, I can't hear anything!
Tja	Expressing resignation or "that's life"	Well	**Tja**, so ist das Leben.	Well, that's life.
Huch	Expressing surprise	Whoa	**Huch**, wo ist mein Handy?	Whoa, where's my phone?
Brr	Expressing cold or chilliness	Brr	**Brr**, es ist kalt draußen!	Brr, it's cold outside!
Puh	Expressing exhaustion or relief	Whew	**Puh**, die Arbeit war anstrengend!	Whew, that work was exhausting!

Interjections are often followed by an exclamation point, but they can also be followed by a comma or a period, depending on the context and the strength of the emotion.

The tone of voice when using an interjection can greatly change its meaning. For example, *Oh!* could express surprise, disappointment, or even sarcasm, depending on how it's said.

Büroausstattung (Office Equipment)	
(der) Schreibtisch	desk
(der) Stuhl	chair
(der) Computer	computer
(die) Tastatur	keyboard
(die) Maus	mouse
(der) Drucker	printer
(das) Telefon	telephone
(der) Bildschirm	monitor/display
(der) Aktenordner	file folder/binder
drucken	(to) print
(das) Papier	paper
(der) Stift	pen
(der) Bleistift	pencil
(die) Notiz	note
(die) Weißwandtafel	whiteboard
(der) Taschenrechner	calculator
(der) Locher	hole punch

Arbeiten in Deutschland: Kulturelle Unterschiede und Herausforderungen (Working in Germany: Cultural Differences and Challenges) – *Wortschatz* (Vocabulary)

zugeben [v.]	(to) admit
arbeiten [v.]	(to) work
anders [adv.]	differently
(die) Integration (-en) [n.]	integration
(der) Zweck (-e) [n.]	purpose
inwiefern [adv.]	to what extent
pünktlich [adj.]	on time
(das) Treffen (-) [n.]	meeting
erscheinen [v.]	(to) appear
höflich [adj.]	courteous
(der) Respekt (-) [n.]	respect
bemerken [v.]	(to) notice
direkt [adv.]	direct
(der) Beginn (-e) [n.]	beginning
überwältigend [adj.]	overwhelming
(das) Missverständnis (-se) [n.]	misunderstanding
vermeiden [v.]	(to) avoid
(wert-)schätzen [v.]	(to) value
(das) Gespräch (-e) [n.]	conversation
(die) Perspektive (-n) [n.]	perspective
(die) Brücke (-n) [n.]	bridge

Work-Life-Balance in Deutschland: Ein Schlüssel zum Glück (Work-Life Balance in Germany: A Key to Happiness) – *Wortschatz* (Vocabulary)

streben [v.]	(to) strive
(das) Gleichgewicht (-e) [n.]	balance
(die) Freizeit (-en) [n.]	leisure
erheblich [adj.]	considerable
(die) Bedeutung (-en) [n.]	importance
(die) Zufriedenheit (-) [n.]	satisfaction
fördern [v.]	(to) promote
steigern [v.]	(to) increase
zufrieden [adj.]	satisfied
(das) Arbeitsergebnis (-se) [n.]	work result
(die) Beförderung (-en) [n.]	promotion
(der) Stellenwert (-e) [n.]	importance
(das) Fitnessstudio (-s) [n.]	gym
genießen [v.]	(to) enjoy
erfrischen [v.]	(to) refresh
täglich [adj.]	daily
richtig [adj.]	properly

Section 2
FORT- UND WEITERBILDUNG
(PROFESSIONAL DEVELOPMENT)

 DIE EINARBEITUNGSZEIT IN EINEM NEUEN LAND
(THE SETTLING-IN PERIOD IN A NEW COUNTRY)

Mark, a new resident in Germany, is eager to learn the language. He approaches Tina, an experienced language instructor, to discuss language courses available in the city. The dialogue covers the specified grammar topics: using „um ... zu" for purposes, the infinitive clause, and the use of „selbst" and „sogar".

Mark: Hallo Tina! Ich bin nach Deutschland gezogen, **um** hier zu arbeiten und **um** die Kultur besser zu verstehen. Aber ich finde, dass ich die Sprache lernen muss, **um** mich richtig zu integrieren.

Tina: Hallo Mark! Es ist wirklich wichtig, die Sprache zu lernen, **wenn** man in einem neuen Land wohnt. Es gibt viele Sprachschulen in der Stadt, die Kurse für Anfänger **bis** Fortgeschrittene anbieten.

Mark: Das klingt gut! Ich möchte **einen Kurs belegen**, **um** meine Kommunikationsfähigkeiten zu verbessern. Wie lange dauert ein solcher Kurs in der Regel?

Tina: Ein Anfängerkurs dauert oft acht Wochen, aber es kommt darauf an, wie intensiv du lernen möchtest. Einige Schüler entscheiden **sich dafür**, **mehr Stunden pro Woche zu nehmen**, **um** schneller voranzukommen.

Mark: Interessant. Ich habe von einem Kurs gehört, der sich nur auf Konversation konzentriert. Ist das auch möglich?

Tina: Ja, das gibt es **sogar** in mehreren Schulen. Der Hauptzweck solcher Kurse ist es, das Sprechen zu fördern und **den Schülern zu helfen, sich im Alltag besser zu verständigen**.

Mark: Und was ist mit Online-Kursen? Ich reise manchmal und möchte flexibel bleiben.

Tina: Viele Schulen bieten **sogar** Online-Optionen an. Du kannst **selbst** entscheiden, ob du den Kurs im Klassenzimmer oder online absolvieren möchtest.

Mark: Das klingt perfekt! Ich werde mich anmelden. Danke für die Informationen, Tina.

Tina: Gern geschehen, Mark. Viel Erfolg beim Lernen!

LEBENSLANGES LERNEN: EIN SCHLÜSSEL ZUR ENTFALTUNG
(LIFELONG LEARNING: A KEY TO UNFOLDING)

*Die ständige Bereitschaft, Neues zu lernen, ist heute unerlässlich. Es hilft nicht nur, **um** beruflich up-to-date zu bleiben, sondern auch **um** sich persönlich weiterzuentwickeln. Viele beginnen zu verstehen, dass es nötig ist, **um** mit den jüngsten technologischen Veränderungen Schritt zu halten.*

*Durch ständige Weiterbildung können wir sicherstellen, dass wir **selbst** in einer sich wandelnden Arbeitslandschaft relevant bleiben. **Sogar** in späteren Lebensphasen entdecken Menschen die Vorteile des Lernens: Es ermöglicht, neue Hobbys zu entwickeln oder verborgene Talente zu erkennen.*

*Es ist spannend zu sehen, wie lebenslanges Lernen es jedem Einzelnen ermöglicht, nicht nur Wissen, sondern auch Weisheit zu sammeln. Es geht darum, ständig bereit zu sein, Neues zu lernen, **um** sich **selbst** und die Welt besser zu verstehen.*

2.1 DIE VERWENDUNG VON „UM ... ZU" FÜR ZWECKE
(USING „UM ... ZU" FOR PURPOSES)

The German phrase „um... zu" is a common and useful construction that translates to "in order to" in English. It's used to express the purpose or the intention behind an action.

Core Concept:

↳ „um ... zu" is used to link two clauses: the main clause, which has the action, and the subordinate clause, which explains the purpose of the action. This construction neatly encapsulates the motive behind an action.

Structure
[Main Clause] + um + [Rest of Subordinate Clause] + [zu + Infinitive Verb]

Examples:

Main Clause:	Sie spart Geld
Purpose (um... zu):	um
Infinitive Verb:	kaufen
Rest of Subordinate Clause:	sich ein neues Auto
Complete Sentence:	Sie spart Geld, um sich ein neues Auto zu kaufen.
Translation:	She is saving money in order to buy a new car.

Main Clause:	*Er lernt täglich*
Purpose (um... zu):	*um*
Infinitive Verb:	*verbessern*
Rest of Subordinate Clause:	*seine Kenntnisse*
Complete Sentence:	*Er lernt täglich, um seine Sprachkenntnisse zu verbessern.*
Translation:	He studies daily in order to improve his language skills.

The „um ... zu" clause can be placed either before or after the main clause, depending on which part the speaker wants to emphasize. However, it's more common to see the main clause first.

Standard Placement (Main Clause First)		
	Example 1	**Example 2**
Main Clause:	*Er nimmt einen Schirm mit,*	*Sie liest viele Bücher,*
***um ... zu* Clause:**	*um sich vor dem Regen zu schützen.*	*um ihr Wissen zu erweitern.*
Complete Sentence:	*Er nimmt einen Schirm mit, um sich vor dem Regen zu schützen.*	*Sie liest viele Bücher, um ihr Wissen zu erweitern.*
Translation:	He takes an umbrella in order to protect himself from the rain.	She reads many books in order to expand her knowledge.

Inverted Placement (Purpose Clause First)		
	Example 1	**Example 2**
***um ... zu* Clause:**	*Um die Umwelt zu schonen,*	*Um ihre Sprachkenntnisse zu verbessern,*
Main Clause:	*fährt er mit dem Fahrrad zur Arbeit.*	*besucht sie einen Deutschkurs.*
Complete Sentence:	*Um die Umwelt zu schonen, fährt er mit dem Fahrrad zur Arbeit.*	*Um ihre Sprachkenntnisse zu verbessern, besucht sie einen Deutschkurs.*
Translation:	In order to preserve the environment, he rides his bike to work.	In order to improve her language skills, she attends a German course.

In these examples, when the „um ... zu" clause comes first, it emphasizes the purpose or reason behind the action. The speaker might choose this order to highlight the motivation before stating what is actually being done. In contrast, the standard placement (main clause first) tends to present the action more straightforwardly, with the purpose following as additional information.

Typically, the subject of both clauses in an „um ... zu" construction is the same. If the subjects of the main clause and the subordinate clause are different, a different construction is generally used.

2.2 DER INFINITIVSATZ (INFINITIVE CLAUSE) ▷ Ü 2.1)

The *Infinitivsatz* (infinitive clause) is a useful structure that uses an infinitive verb to add information to a main clause, often explaining the reason, manner, or purpose of an action. These clauses are versatile and can provide concise yet detailed insights into actions or events.

An infinitive clause in German typically consists of an infinitive verb often combined with „zu". It's used to give more information about the action described in the main clause. These clauses are frequently used after certain verbs, adjectives, and nouns, and can be instrumental in expressing a wide range of nuances and details in a sentence.

The basic structure of an infinitive clause is as follows:

Structure
[Main Clause] + [Infinitive Verb with „zu"]

The infinitive verb is usually placed at the end of the clause.

Examples and Usage:

With Verbs	
Main Clause:	*Er versucht*
Infinitive Clause:	*schnell **zu laufen**.*
Complete Sentence:	*Er versucht, schnell **zu laufen**.*
Translation:	He tries to run quickly.

With Adjectives	
Main Clause:	*Es ist wichtig*
Infinitive Clause:	*genug **zu schlafen**.*
Complete Sentence:	*Es ist wichtig, genug **zu schlafen**.*
Translation:	It is important to sleep enough.

With Nouns	
Main Clause:	*Sie hat die Chance*
Infinitive Clause:	*im Ausland **zu studieren**.*
Complete Sentence:	*Sie hat die Chance, im Ausland **zu studieren**.*
Translation:	She has the opportunity to study abroad.

Special Cases and Variations:

Separable Prefix Verbs:

↳ With separable prefix verbs, „zu" is placed between the prefix and the base verb.
Example: *Er fängt an, das Zimmer aufzuräumen.* (He begins to clean up the room.)

Infinitive Clauses without 'zu':

↳ After certain verbs like modal verbs or „lassen", „sehen", „hören", „fühlen" and „helfen" the infinitive is used without „zu".
Example: *Ich sehe ihn gehen.* (I see him go.)

Infinitive Clause as a Subject or Object:

↳ An infinitive clause can also function as the subject or object of a sentence.
Subject Example: *Zu spät zu kommen, ist unhöflich.* (Being late is impolite.)
Object Example: *Er mag es, am Strand zu liegen.* (He likes lying on the beach.)

The positioning of the infinitive clause can vary for emphasis. Placing it before the main clause highlights the purpose or reason.

Example:

Purpose (Infinitive Clause)	Täglich zu joggen,
Main Clause	hilft ihm, seine Gesundheit zu fördern.
Complete Sentence	Täglich zu joggen, hilft ihm, seine Gesundheit zu fördern.
Translation	Jogging daily helps him to promote his health.

In this sentence, „Täglich zu joggen" (Jogging daily) is positioned at the beginning to emphasize the action of jogging as the primary method for promoting health, before elaborating on its benefit in the main clause.

Kompetenzen und Fähigkeiten (Skills and Abilities)	
lernen	(to) learn
(die) Sprachkenntnisse	language skills
kommunizieren	(to) communicate
(das) Zuhören	listening
schreiben	(to) write
planen	(to) plan
designen	(to) design
(die) Problemlösung	problem-solving
organisieren	(to) organize
(die) Teamarbeit	teamwork
leiten	(to) lead
(das) Verhandeln	negotiating
präsentieren	(to) present
(die) Kreativität	creativity
programmieren	(to) program (computers)
(das) Planen	planning

Arbeitsmarkt (Job Market)	
(die) Arbeit	job
(die) Arbeitsstelle	job position
arbeiten	(to) work
(der) Arbeitgeber	employer
(die) Arbeitnehmerin	employee (female)
(der) Lebenslauf	resume/CV
sich bewerben	(to) apply
(die) Bewerbung	application
(das) Vorstellungsgespräch	job interview
einstellen	(to) hire
kündigen	(to) quit/terminate
(der) Vertrag	contract
(das) Gehalt	salary
(die) Teilzeit	part-time
(die) Vollzeit	full-time
(die) Überstunde	overtime
bezahlen	(to) pay
(die) Stellenanzeige	job advertisement
(das) Praktikum	internship

Die Einarbeitungszeit in einem neuen Land (The settling-in period in a new country) – *Wortschatz* (Vocabulary)

herziehen [v.]	(to) move here
verstehen [v.]	(to) understand
integrieren [v.]	(to) integrate
neu [adj.]	new
(die) Sprachschule (-n) [n.]	language school
(der) Kurs (-e) [n.]	course
(der) Anfänger (-) [n.]	beginner
(der) Fortgeschrittene (-n) [n.]	advanced
verbessern [v.]	(to) improve
belegen [v.]	(to) occupy
verständigen [v.]	(to) communicate
(der) Schüler (-n) [n.]	student
absolvieren [v.]	(to) graduate
konzentriert [adj.]	concentrate
anmelden [v.]	(to) enroll
(der) Erfolg (-e) [n.]	success

Lebenslanges Lernen: Ein Schlüssel zur Entfaltung (Lifelong Learning: A Key to Unfolding) – *Wortschatz* (Vocabulary)

ständig [adj.]	constant
sicherstellen [v.]	(to) ensure
sich wandelnd [adj.]	changing
persönlich [adj.]	personal
weiterentwickeln [v.]	(to) develop/evolve
nötig [adj.]	necessary
technologisch [adj.]	technological
(die) Veränderung (-en) [n.]	change
verborgen [adj.]	hidden
(das) Talent (-e) [n.]	talent
lebenslang [adj.]	lifelong
ermöglichen [v.]	(to) enable
(die) Weisheit (-en) [n.]	wisdom
(das) Wissen (-) [n.]	knowledge
bereit [adj.]	ready
besser [adv.]	better

Section 3
DAS BILDUNGSSYSTEM IN DEUTSCHLAND ERKUNDEN
(EXPLORING GERMANY'S EDUCATION LANDSCAPE)

 STUDIEREN AN DEUTSCHEN UNIVERSITÄTEN
(STUDYING AT GERMAN UNIVERSITIES)

Frank and Carina, both students, meet at a café near their university in Germany. They discuss their experiences and challenges while studying at German universities.

Frank: *Hey Carina, wie läuft dein Studium am **Sprachenzentrum** der Universität?*

Carina: *Es ist ziemlich intensiv, Frank. Besonders die **Sprachkurse** für Fortgeschrittene fordern mich heraus. Und wie steht's mit deinem **Hauptfach**, der **Biotechnologie**?*

Frank: *Ach, die Laborarbeiten und die **Forschungsprojekte** nehmen viel Zeit in Anspruch. Aber es macht Spaß. Hast du schon deinen **Mentoren** an der Fakultät getroffen?*

Carina: *Ja, ich hatte ein Treffen mit Herrn Schmidt, meinem **Forschungsmentor**. Er hat mir wertvolle Tipps für meine **Masterarbeit** gegeben.*

Frank: *Das ist toll! Ich muss auch bald meinen Betreuer für meine **Abschlussarbeit** kontaktieren.*

Carina: *Übrigens, wie findest du die **Bibliothek**? Ich finde den **Lesesaal** dort extrem hilfreich für meine **Literaturrecherche**.*

Frank: *Ja, die **Bibliotheksausstattung** ist wirklich beeindruckend. Vor allem die **Arbeitsgruppenräume** sind super für Teamprojekte.*

Carina: *Absolut. Ich glaube, an deutschen Universitäten gibt es viele Ressourcen, die uns beim Lernen unterstützen.*

Frank: *Da stimme ich dir voll und ganz zu, Carina. Es ist eine Herausforderung, aber auch eine großartige Erfahrung.*

3.1 ZUSAMMENGESETZTE NOMEN (COMPOUND NOUNS)

Ü 3.1)

Compound nouns are formed by combining two or more existing nouns (or other parts of speech) into a single, new noun. The meaning of a compound noun is often (but not always) a combination or a function of its parts.

Structure
[Noun 1] + [Noun 2 (or other parts of speech)] → [New Compound Noun]

A classic example is the combination of „Zahn" (tooth) and „Arzt" (doctor), forming „Zahnarzt" (dentist). In this construction, the last noun „Arzt" determines the compound noun's gender, which is masculine in this case.

Noun 1	Noun 2	Compound Noun	Translation
Zahn (tooth)	Arzt (doctor)	Zahnarzt	Dentist
Geburt (birth)	Tag (day)	Geburtstag	Birthday
Wasser (water)	Flasche (bottle)	Wasserflasche	Water Bottle

At times, an **adjective** and a **noun** might come together to form a compound noun, like „Hochhaus" (high-rise building), where „hoch" (high) combines with „Haus" (house).

Adjective + Noun Combinations	
Kleinkind (toddler, small child)	*Hochgeschwindigkeit* (High-speed)
Klein (small) + *Kind* (child) → *Kleinkind*	*Hoch* (high) + *Geschwindigkeit* (speed) → *Hochgeschwindigkeit*
Meaning: Refers to a very young child, typically between infancy and preschool age.	**Meaning:** Describing something involving high speed.
Example in a sentence: *Kleinkinder brauchen viel Aufmerksamkeit und eine sichere Umgebung.*	**Example in a sentence:** *Der ICE fährt auf bestimmten Strecken mit Hochgeschwindigkeit und verkürzt dadurch die Reisezeit erheblich.*
Translation: Toddlers need a lot of attention and a safe environment.	**Translation:** The ICE travels at high speed on certain routes, thereby significantly reducing travel time.

Combining a **verb** with a **noun** is a less common form but still prevalent, such as „Fernsehen" (television), combining „*fern*" (far) and „*sehen*" (to see).

Verb + Noun Combinations	
Laufband (Treadmill)	*Fahrkarte* (Ticket)
Laufen (to run) + *Band* (belt, strip) → *Laufband*	*Fahren* (to drive/travel) + *Karte* (card, ticket) → *Fahrkarte*
Meaning: Exercise equipment for running or walking in place.	**Meaning:** A ticket for travel, typically for public transport.
Example in a sentence: *Ich benutze im Fitnessstudio täglich das Laufband.*	**Example in a sentence:** *Du musst eine Fahrkarte kaufen, bevor du den Zug betrittst.*
Translation: I use the treadmill daily at the gym.	**Translation:** You need to buy a ticket before you board the train.

A unique aspect of German compound nouns is the occasional use of a linking sound („*Fugenlaut*"), like '*s*' or '*es*', to facilitate smoother pronunciation. This linking sound is not universally applied and often follows regional or customary usage patterns.

Geburt (birth) + *Tag* (day) → *Geburtstag*
Meaning: The day of birth, birthday.

Unlike English, where compound nouns can be written separately, German compound nouns are always written as one continuous word. This characteristic sometimes leads to notably lengthy words, a distinctive feature of the German language.

Sprache (language) + *Wissenschaft* (science) + *Forschung* (research) + *Bibliothek* (library) + *Katalogisierung* (cataloging) + *System* (system) + *Entwicklung* (development)
→ *Sprachwissenschaftsforschungsbibliothekskatalogisierungssystementwicklung*

<u>Meaning:</u> The development of a system for cataloging a library's language science research materials.

Use in a Sentence:

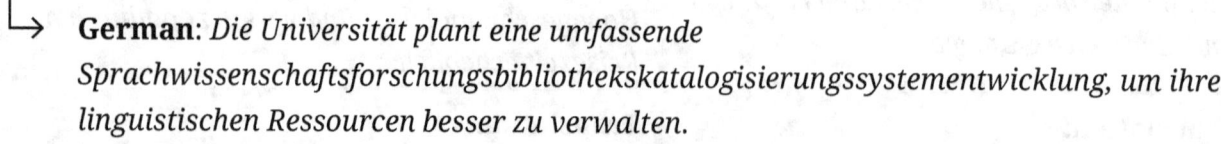 **German:** *Die Universität plant eine umfassende Sprachwissenschaftsforschungsbibliothekskatalogisierungssystementwicklung, um ihre linguistischen Ressourcen besser zu verwalten.*

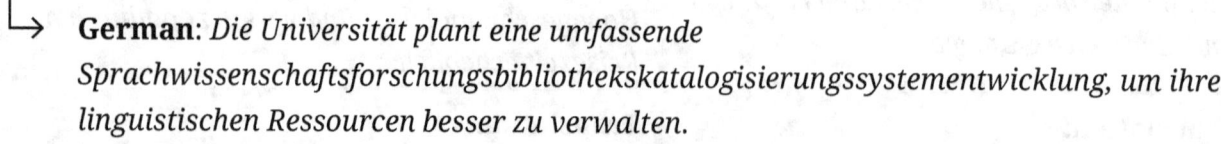 **Translation:** The university is planning a comprehensive development of a system for cataloging its library's language science research materials in order to better manage its linguistic resources.

3.2 N-DEKLINATION (N-DECLENSION)

The N-declension in German grammar is a special category of noun declension that primarily affects masculine nouns. It is characterized by the addition of an *-n* or *-en* to the noun in all cases except the nominative singular.

Structure	
Nominative Singular:	[Noun]
Genitive Singular:	[Noun] + (n/en)
Dative Singular:	[Noun] + (n/en)
Accusative Singular:	[Noun] + (n/en)

Examples:

Noun (Singular)	Nominative	Genitive	Dative	Accusative
der Junge	*der Junge*	*des Junge**n***	*dem Junge**n***	*den Junge**n***
der Student	*der Student*	*des Student**en***	*dem Student**en***	*den Student**en***
der Herr	*der Herr*	*des Herr**n***	*dem Herr**n***	*den Herr**n***

Many nouns of foreign origin, particularly those ending in *-ant, -ent, -ist, -oge,* and *-om,* undergo N-declension.

Noun (Singular)	Nominative	Genitive	Dative	Accusative
Tourist (tourist)	der Tourist	des Tourist**en**	dem Tourist**en**	den Tourist**en**

Some common nouns like '*Herz*' (heart) and '*Held*' (hero), despite not ending in *-e*, follow this declension pattern.

Noun (Singular)	Nominative	Genitive	Dative	Accusative
Held (hero)	der Held	des Held**ens**	dem Held**en**	den Held**en**
Herz (heart)	das Herz	des Herz**ens**	dem Herz**en**	das Herz

Nouns ending in *-el, -er, -en*: These do not typically follow N-declension.

Noun (Singular)	Nominative	Genitive	Dative	Accusative
Leh**rer** (teacher)	der Lehrer	des Lehrers	dem Lehrer	den Lehrer
Vog**el** (bird)	der Vogel	des Vogels	dem Vogel	den Vogel

Some nouns can be declined either way, following regular declension or N-declension.

Noun (Singular)	Nominative	Genitive	Dative	Accusative
Bauer (farmer)	der Bauer	des Bauers	dem Bauer	den Bauer
Bauer (farmer)	der Bauer	des Bauern	dem Bauern	den Bauern

Studiengänge und Fächer (Fields of Study and Subjects)	
Betriebswirtschaftslehre	Business Administration
Informatik	Computer Science
Maschinenbau	Mechanical Engineering
Elektrotechnik	Electrical Engineering
Medizin	Medicine
Jura	Law
Psychologie	Psychology
Biologie	Biology
Chemie	Chemistry
Physik	Physics
Soziologie	Sociology
Politikwissenschaft	Political Science
Geschichte	History
Philosophie	Philosophy
Kunst	Art
Musikwissenschaft	Musicology
Architektur	Architecture
Bauingenieurwesen	Civil Engineering
Umweltwissenschaften	Environmental Sciences
Volkswirtschaftslehre	Economics
Mathematik	Mathematics
Englische Literatur	English Literature
Germanistik	German Studies

Studieren an deutschen Universitäten (Studying at German universities) – Wortschatz (Vocabulary)

(das) Studium (Studien) [n.]	study
(das) Sprachenzentrum (Sprachenzentren) [n.]	language center
intensiv [adj.]	intensive
(das) Hauptfach (Hauptfächer) [n.]	main subject
herausfordern [v.]	(to) challenge
(die) Laborarbeit (-en) [n.]	lab work
in Anspruch nehmen [v.]	(to) make use of
(das) Treffen (-) [n.]	meeting
wertvoll [adj.]	valuable
(die) Fakultät (-en) [n.]	faculty
(der) Betreuer (-) [n.]	supervisor
(die) Masterarbeit (-en) [n.]	Master's thesis
hilfreich [adj.]	helpful
(die) Bibliothek (-en) [n.]	library
(die) Ausstattung (-en) [n.]	equipment
(die) Literaturrecherche (-n) [n.]	literature research
(die) Ressource (-n) [n.]	resource
(die) Herausforderung (-en) [n.]	challenge
(das) Projekt (-e) [n.]	project

ÜBUNGEN (EXERCISES)

Ü 1.1) Bestimme, ob es sich bei dem folgenden Satz um einen Finalsatz oder einen Kausalsatz handelt und ergänze ihn entsprechend. Verwende „*damit*" für **Finalsätze** und „*weil*" für **Kausalsätze**.

Determine whether the following sentence is a purpose clause (*Finalsatz*) or a cause clause (*Kausalsatz*) and complete it accordingly. Use „*damit*" for purpose clauses and „*weil*" for cause clauses.

Example: Ich nehme einen Regenschirm mit, _____ ich nicht nass werde.
Antwort: Finalsatz - Ich nehme einen Regenschirm mit, **damit** ich nicht nass werde.

a. Er lernt viel, _____ er die Prüfung besteht. _____

b. Sie trägt einen Hut, _____ die Sonne sehr stark ist. _____

c. Wir gehen früh schlafen, _____ wir morgen früh aufstehen müssen. _____

d. Sie nimmt ein Medikament, _____ sie Kopfschmerzen hat. _____

e. Er spart Geld, _____ er sich ein neues Auto kaufen kann. _____

f. Sie zieht einen Mantel an, _____ es draußen kalt ist. _____

g. Wir machen das Fenster auf, _____ frische Luft hereinkommt. _____

h. Er isst nichts Süßes, _____ er abnehmen kann. _____

i. Sie ruft an, _____ sie Informationen benötigt. _____

j. Er trägt Sonnencreme auf, _____ er keinen Sonnenbrand bekommt. _____

Ü. 1.2) Verwandle die vorgegebenen Verben in Nomen. Achte darauf, dass das resultierende Nomen großgeschrieben wird. Bilde zusätzlich einen Satz mit dem nominalisierten Verb.

Change the given verbs into nouns. Remember to capitalize the resulting noun. Also, form a sentence using the nominalized verb.

Example: **Verb:** tanzen
Nominalisiert: Das Tanzen
Satz: Das Tanzen am Abend war sehr schön.

a. lernen _____ _____

b. spielen _____ _____

c. reisen _____ _____

d. singen _____ _____

e. arbeiten _____ _____

f. kochen _____ _____

g. leben _____ _____

h. schreiben _____ _____

Ü 1.3) Wandle die folgenden Sätze so um, dass das Verb als Nomen erscheint. Beachte dabei, dass der Satz in seiner Bedeutung gleichbleiben soll.
Transform the following sentences so that the verb appears as a nominalized noun. Ensure that the sentence retains its original meaning.

Example: *Satz:* „Sie liebt es zu reisen."

Nominalisiert: „Sie liebt **das Reisen**."

a. Es ist wichtig, regelmäßig zu üben.
_____

b. Er hofft, bald wieder gesund zu werden.
_____

c. Sie vermeidet es, nachts alleine zu laufen.
_____

d. Er genießt es, Gitarre zu spielen.
_____

e. Es ist schwer, früh aufzustehen.
_____

f. Sie versucht, schneller zu laufen.
_____

g. Er plant, nächstes Jahr zu studieren.
_____

Ü 1.4) Ergänze die folgenden Dialoge oder Sätze mit passenden Interjektionen. Achte darauf, dass die Interjektionen den Emotionen oder Reaktionen in den Sätzen entsprechen.

Complete the following dialogues or sentences with appropriate interjections. Make sure the interjections match the emotions or reactions in the sentences.

Example:

„_____, das war knapp!", sagte er, nachdem er fast hingefallen wäre.

Antwort: „_Uff_, das war knapp!"

a. „_____, ich habe den Zug verpasst!", sagte sie enttäuscht.

b. „_____, was für eine Überraschung, dich hier zu sehen!", rief er aus.

c. „_____, das Essen schmeckt fantastisch!", lobte er den Koch.

d. „_____, ich habe mein Portemonnaie zu Hause vergessen!", bemerkte sie.

e. „_____, das ist ja ein niedlicher Hund!", sagte das Kind.

Ü 2.1) Ergänze die Sätze mit einem passenden Infinitivsatz. Achte darauf, dass der Infinitivsatz sinnvoll in den Kontext des Hauptsatzes passt.

Complete the sentences with an appropriate infinitive clause. Ensure that the infinitive clause fits logically into the context of the main sentence.

Example: *Satz:* Es ist wichtig, _____.

Ergänzung: Es ist wichtig, genug Wasser zu trinken.

a. Sie versucht, _____.

b. Er hat keine Zeit, _____.

c. Es ist nicht leicht, _____.

d. Wir planen, _____.

e. Es macht Spaß, _____.

f. Sie hofft, _____.

Ü 3.1) Bilde zusammengesetzte Nomen, indem du die Wörter aus der linken Spalte mit einem passenden Wort aus der mittleren Spalte kombinierst. Notiere das zusammengesetzte Nomen in der rechten Spalte.

Create compound nouns by combining a word from the left column with a suitable word from the middle column. Write down the compound noun in the right column.

Example:

Wort 1	Wort 2	Zusammengesetztes Nomen
Zahn	Bürste	Zahnbürste

Wort 1	Wort 2	Zusammengesetztes Nomen
Schlaf	Zimmer	
Kinder	Garten	
Buch	Regal	
Kaffee	Tasse	
Blumen	Vase	
Wasser	Flasche	
Straßen	Laterne	
Auto	Bahn	
Stadt	Plan	

Unit 6

HOBBYS UND FREIZEIT

(HOBBIES AND LEISURE TIME)

Unit VI, „Hobbys und Freizeit", is all about exploring the German language through leisure activities and hobbies. In the first section, „Sportliche Aktivitäten", you'll engage with language related to sports and physical hobbies, focusing on sentence structure and temporal phrases to describe activities and events. This section offers a fun and interactive way to learn German while talking about popular sports and hobbies. Moving on to „Musik und Kunst", the unit dives into the artistic realm, teaching you how to express opinions and experiences related to music and art. Here, you'll learn about direct speech, temporal clauses, and specific vocabulary related to the arts. This unit is designed to not only enhance your language skills but also to connect your learning experience with enjoyable and relatable topics, making German more accessible and engaging.

Section 1

SPORTLICHE AKTIVITÄTEN
(SPORTS ACTIVITIES)

 FUSSBALLFIEBER IN DEUTSCHLAND
(SOCCER FEVER IN GERMANY)

Jasmin and Benedikt are in a park in Germany, kicking a soccer ball around. They are both avid soccer fans, but support rival teams. Their conversation is filled with playful banter.

Jasmin:	**Bevor** wir weitermachen, muss ich wissen: Für welchen Verein bist du denn?
Benedikt:	Für Bayern München natürlich. Und du?
Jasmin:	Borussia Dortmund! Ich kann es kaum glauben, dass ich mit einem Bayern-Fan Fußball spiele.
Benedikt:	Das ist ja wie ein Löwe, der mit einer Katze spielt! Aber **nachdem** wir beide Fußball lieben, ist das wohl okay.
Jasmin:	Ja, solange du, **bevor** wir anfangen zu spielen, dein Bayern-Trikot versteckst.
Benedikt:	Nur wenn du, **nachdem** wir fertig sind, zugibst, dass Bayern besser ist.
Jasmin:	Das wird nie passieren! **Bevor** ich das sage, können Schweine fliegen!
Benedikt:	Okay, dann lass uns spielen. Aber **nachdem** ich das letzte Tor geschossen habe, feiern wir mit einem Bier – auf meine Kosten.
Jasmin:	Abgemacht! Aber **bevor** wir starten, eine kleine Warnung: Ich spiele wie Marco Reus.
Benedikt:	Und ich verteidige wie Manuel Neuer. Das wird ein spannendes Spiel!

1.1 SATZGLIEDER UND SATZSTRUKTUR   ▷ Ü 1.1), 1.2)
(SENTENCE COMPONENTS AND SENTENCE STRUCTURE)

Understanding the components of a sentence (*Satzglieder*) and the structure (*Satzstruktur*) in German is crucial for both comprehension and correct language use. This section delves deeper into the components that make up a German sentence and how they are typically structured.

Subject (Subjekt)	Predicate (Prädikat)	Direct Object (Akkusativobjekt)	Indirect Object (Dativobjekt)	Adverbial Determinatives (Adverbiale Bestimmungen)
The actor or topic of the sentence.	The verb or verb phrase that describes the action or state.	The recipient of the action, usually in the accusative case.	Typically in the dative case, it often indicates to whom or for whom the action is done.	Provide additional information such as time, manner, place, cause, etc.
Example: „Der Hund (The dog)" in „Der Hund bellt."	Example: „bellt (barks)" in „Der Hund bellt."	Example: „den Ball (the ball)" in „Der Hund jagt den Ball."	Example: „dem Kind (the child)" in „Der Hund folgt dem Kind."	Examples: „schnell (quickly)" for manner. „im Park (in the park)" for place. „jeden Tag (every day)" for time.

German sentence structure varies between main and subordinate clauses. The 'Verb Second' (V2) rule is a key feature in main clauses, whereas subordinate clauses typically follow a 'Verb Last' structure.

Main Clause Structure:

↳ The finite verb is always in the second position, but other elements can move around for emphasis.

Basic Order
Subject + Predicate + Object + Adverbials

Subject	Predicate	Direct Object	Adverbial
Der Hund	jagt	den Ball	im Park.
(The dog)	(chases)	(the ball)	(in the park.)

Subordinate Clause Structure:

↳ Introduced by subordinating conjunctions (e.g., *dass, weil, wenn*).
   The conjugated verb is placed at the end of the clause.

Subordinating Conjunction	Subject	Object	Predicate
weil	der Hund	den Ball	jagt.
(because)	(the dog)	(the ball)	(chases)

The flexibility of German sentence structure allows for emphasizing different parts of a sentence by rearranging its components, especially in spoken language.

Standard: „*Ich esse **jeden Tag** Obst.*"
Emphasis on time: „***Jeden Tag** esse ich Obst.*"

Adverbial (Time)	Predicate	Subject	Object
Jeden Tag	*esse*	*ich*	*Obst.*
(Every day)	(eat)	(I)	(fruit).

1.2 DIE VERWENDUNG VON „BEVOR" UND „NACHDEM"
(USING „BEVOR" AND „NACHDEM")

„*Bevor*" and „*nachdem*" are subordinating conjunctions used to express temporal relationships between two events. „*Bevor*" translates to "before", and „*nachdem*" translates to "after".

„*Bevor*" (Before):

↳ „*Bevor*" is used to indicate that one action occurs before another. The clause introduced by „*bevor*" is a subordinate clause.

In sentences with „***bevor***", the conjugated verb in the subordinate clause moves to the end.

Example:

Ich esse immer, ***bevor*** *ich zur Arbeit* <u>*gehe*</u>*.*
Translation: I always eat before I go to work.

Structure
[Main Clause],   *bevor*   [Subordinate Clause]

The subordinate clause introduced by „***bevor***" follows the '<u>Verb Last</u>' rule.

Example:

Bevor *wir den Film* <u>*sehen*</u>*, kaufen wir Popcorn.*
(Before we watch the movie, we buy popcorn.)

„Nachdem" (After):

↳ „Nachdem" is used to indicate that one action occurs after another. It introduces a subordinate clause.

Similar to „*bevor*", the <u>verb</u> in the „*nachdem*" clause is placed at the end.

Example:

Nachdem ich aufgestanden <u>war</u>, machte ich Frühstück.
(After I had gotten up, I made breakfast.)

Structure
Nachdem [Subordinate Clause], [Main Clause].

The verb in the subordinate clause introduced by „*nachdem*" is also positioned last.

Example:

Wir gingen spazieren, nachdem wir zu Mittag gegessen hatten.
Translation: We went for a walk after we had lunch.

Sportliche Aktivitäten (Sports Activities)	
joggen	(to) jog
Fußball spielen	(to) play soccer/football
schwimmen	(to) swim
Rad fahren	(to) cycle
wandern	(to) hike
Tennis spielen	(to) play tennis
Basketball spielen	(to) play basketball
Golf spielen	(to) play golf
Ski fahren	(to) ski
Snowboard fahren	(to) snowboard
Yoga machen	(to) do yoga
Pilates machen	(to) do Pilates
Gewichte heben	(to) lift weights
boxen	(to) box
laufen	(to) run

Künstlerische Tätigkeiten (Artistic Activities)	
malen	(to) paint
zeichnen	(to) draw
fotografieren	(to) photograph
töpfern	(to) do pottery
Bildhauerei betreiben	(to) sculpt
tanzen	(to) dance
Theater spielen	(to) act in theater
komponieren	(to) compose music
Gedichte verfassen	(to) write poetry
weben	(to) weave
sticken	(to) embroider

Fußballfieber in Deutschland (Soccer Fever in Germany) – *Wortschatz* (Vocabulary)

weitermachen [v.]	(to) continue
(der) Verein (-e) [n.]	club
solange [conj.]	as long as
wohl [adv.]	well
verstecken [v.]	(to) hide
zugeben [v.]	(to) admit
(das) Trikot (-s) [n.]	jersey
fliegen [v.]	(to) fly
(das) Schwein (-e) [n.]	pig
(das) Tor (-e) [n.]	goal
schießen [v.]	(to) shoot
feiern [v.]	(to) celebrate
(das) Bier (-e) [n.]	beer
auf meine Kosten [expr.]	at my expense
(die) Warnung (-en) [n.]	warning
verteidigen [v.]	(to) defend

Section 2
MUSIK UND KUNST
(MUSIC AND ART)

 DER KÜNSTLERISCHE REIZ BERLINS
(BERLIN'S ARTISTIC CHARM)

Luisa and Leon visit an art museum in Berlin. They wander through the various exhibitions, commenting on the artwork and discussing their plans for the day.

Luisa: Siehst du dieses Gemälde, Leon? Es sieht so realistisch aus, als könnte man in die Szene hineintreten.

Leon: Wirklich beeindruckend. Der Künstler sagte einmal in einem Interview, dass er so lange an einem Bild malt, **bis** es fast lebendig wirkt.

Luisa: Solange wir hier sind, sollten wir auch die moderne Kunstausstellung besuchen. Ich habe gehört, dass sie sehr interessant sein soll.

Leon: Gute Idee! Ich habe gelesen, dass sie eine interaktive Installation haben, bei der man Teil des Kunstwerks wird. Das müssen wir sehen!

Luisa: Ja, und vergiss nicht, dass wir um 17 Uhr im Café mit Anna und Jonas verabredet sind und **bis** dahin fertig sein müssen.

Leon: Stimmt, ich erinnere mich. Anna sagte, sie würde uns dort treffen, **solange** der Verkehr nicht zu schlimm ist.

Luisa: Hoffentlich haben wir genug Zeit, alles zu sehen. Ich möchte besonders die Skulpturengalerie nicht verpassen.

Leon: Keine Sorge, wir schaffen das schon. Und solange wir zusammen sind, wird es sicher ein toller Tag.

2.1 DIE DIREKTE REDE
(DIRECT SPEECH)

▷ Ü 2.1)

Direct speech is used to report the exact words said by a speaker. It is typically enclosed in quotation marks and is often accompanied by a reporting verb.

> "Auf keinen Fall!" → *Das doppelte Strichlein ist kein Anführungszeichen!*
>
> "Yes, if English!" → *Die korrekte englische Variante*
>
> „So soll's sein!" → *Im Deutschen bitte so*

In German, direct speech is typically enclosed within lower quotation marks („) at the beginning and upper quotation marks (") at the end.

↳ *Sie sagte: „Ich freue mich auf das Wochenende."*
Translation: She said, "I am looking forward to the weekend."

Commas are used to separate the direct speech from the reporting clause.

↳ *Er antwortete: „Ja, ich habe den Brief bereits geschrieben."*
Translation: He replied, "Yes, I have already written the letter."

The first letter of the direct speech sentence is always capitalized.

↳ *Der Lehrer fragte: „Habt ihr eure Hausaufgaben gemacht?"*
Translation: The teacher asked, "Have you done your homework?"

When the direct speech is a question, the question mark is placed inside the quotation marks.

↳ *Er fragte: „Wann beginnt der Film?"*
Translation: He asked, "When does the movie start?"

Exclamatory sentences within direct speech also keep their exclamation marks inside the quotation marks.

↳ *Sie rief: „Achtung, der Zug kommt!"*
Translation: She exclaimed, "Watch out, the train is coming!"

In dialogues, each new line of direct speech from a different speaker starts with a new paragraph.

„Kannst du mir helfen?", fragte Peter.
„Natürlich, worum geht es?", antwortete Maria.
Translation: "Can you help me?" asked Peter.
"Of course, what's it about?" Maria replied.

2.2 TEMPORALSÄTZE MIT „SOLANGE" UND „BIS"
(TEMPORAL CLAUSES WITH „SOLANGE" AND „BIS")

In German grammar, temporal clauses using „solange" and „bis" are instrumental in expressing time-related aspects of actions. „Solange" translates to "as long as" and is used to indicate the continuation of an action under certain conditions. In contrast, „bis", meaning "until", denotes the point in time up to which an action extends. These temporal clauses are not merely functional elements; they play a significant role in clarifying the circumstances under which actions occur, their duration, and the specific conditions affecting them.

Usage of *"solange"*	Usage of *"bis"*
„Solange" is used to describe a condition under which an action takes place. It emphasizes the duration or the condition that needs to be met for the action to occur or continue.	„Bis" is used to indicate the point in time until which an action continues. It sets a boundary or a limit for the duration of the action.
Example: Solange du hier bist, fühle ich mich sicher. (As long as you are here, I feel safe.)	**Example:** Ich werde hier warten, bis du zurückkommst. (I will wait here until you come back.) The action of waiting will continue until the condition of the other person returning is met.

„Solange" is often used to emphasize that as long as a certain condition exists, the action will continue.

Situation:	Imagine someone studying as long as it's quiet.
German:	Solange es ruhig ist, studiert sie.
Translation:	As long as it is quiet, she studies.
Explanation:	Here, „solange" sets a condition (quietness) for the action (studying) to continue. The studying is ongoing, contingent on the quiet environment.

„Bis" sets a specific endpoint for an action, indicating that the action will cease once a particular point in time is reached or a condition is met.

Situation:	Someone plans to study until midnight.
German:	*Sie studiert bis Mitternacht.*
Translation:	She studies until midnight.
Explanation:	In this sentence, „*bis*" specifies the endpoint of the action (studying). The studying will stop when it reaches midnight.

Interplay Between „*Solange*" and „*Bis*":

Situation:	A scenario where someone studies as long as it's quiet but only until their friend arrives.
German:	*Solange es ruhig ist, studiert sie, bis ihr Freund ankommt.*
Translation:	As long as it is quiet, she studies until her friend arrives.
Explanation:	This sentence combines both aspects. The action (studying) is ongoing due to the condition of quietness („*solange*") but has a clear endpoint, which is the arrival of her friend („*bis*").

The interplay of „*solange*" and „*bis*" in a single sentence can effectively communicate both the condition for an action's continuation and its eventual endpoint.

Musikalische Hobbys (Musical Hobbies)	
ein Instrument spielen	(to) play an instrument
Klavier spielen	(to) play the piano
Gitarre spielen	(to) play the guitar
Schlagzeug spielen	(to) play the drums
Geige spielen	(to) play the violin
Saxofon spielen	(to) play the saxophone
singen	(to) sing
einen Song schreiben	(to) write a song
Musik aufnehmen	(to) record music
Platten auflegen	(to) DJ

Der künstlerische Reiz Berlins (Berlin's artistic charm) – *Wortschatz* (Vocabulary)

(das) Gemälde (-) [n.]	painting
realistisch [adj.]	realistic
(die) Szene (-n) [n.]	scene
hineintreten [v.]	(to) enter
malen [v.]	(to) paint
fast [adv.]	almost
lebendig [adj.]	vivid
wirken [v.]	(to) appear
(die) Kunstausstellung (-en) [n.]	art exhibition
interaktiv [adj.]	interactive
(das) Kunstwerk (-e) [n.]	artwork
vergessen [v.]	(to) forget
verabreden [v.]	(to) arrange
schlimm [adj.]	bad
(der) Verkehr (-e) [n.]	traffic
(die) Skulptur (-en) [n.]	sculpture
(die) Galerie (-n) [n.]	gallery
verpassen [v.]	(to) miss
schaffen [v.]	(to) create

ÜBUNGEN (EXERCISES)

Ü 1.1) Untersuche die gegebenen Sätze und bestimme die Satzglieder (Subjekt, Prädikat, Objekt, Adverbiale). Danach stelle die Sätze um, um eine neue, korrekte Satzstruktur zu bilden.
Examine the given sentences and identify the components of the sentence (subject, predicate, object, adverbials). Then, rearrange the sentences to form a new, correct sentence structure.

Example:　　*Originalsatz:*　　„Der schnelle Hund jagt den roten Ball."

　　　　　　　Satzglieder:　　　**Subjekt:**　Der schnelle Hund
　　　　　　　　　　　　　　　　Prädikat:　jagt
　　　　　　　　　　　　　　　　Objekt:　　den roten Ball

　　　　　　　Umgestellter Satz:　„Den roten Ball jagt der schnelle Hund."

a. „Die Kinder spielen im Garten Fußball."

_____

_____

b. „Der talentierte Musiker spielt eine schöne Melodie auf seiner Geige."

_____

_____

c. „Sie trifft alte Freunde in Berlin."

_____

_____

d. „Der alte Mann liest jeden Morgen in der Bibliothek die Zeitung."

_____

_____

Ü 1.2) Analysiere die gegebenen Sätze in der Tabelle und bestimme die Satzglieder: Subjekt, Prädikat, Objekt, und Adverbiale. Trage die Satzglieder in die entsprechenden Spalten der Tabelle ein.
Analyze the given sentences in the table and identify the sentence components: subject, predicate, object, and adverbials. Fill in the corresponding columns of the table with these components.

Example:

Satz	Subjekt	Prädikat	Objekt	Adverbiale
Ich esse schmatzend Kuchen.	Ich	esse	Kuchen	schmatzend

Satz	Subjekt	Prädikat	Objekt	Adverbiale
Das Auto fährt schnell.				
Kinder lachen im Park.				
Maria kauft im Supermarkt ein neues Buch.				
Der Lehrer erklärt die Aufgabe in der Schule.				
Wir gehen heute ins Kino.				

Ü 2.1) Wandle die folgenden Sätze in direkte Rede um. Achte darauf, die korrekten Satzzeichen und die Einleitung der direkten Rede zu verwenden.

Transform the following sentences into direct speech. Be sure to use the correct punctuation and introduce the direct speech properly.

Example: Er sagte, dass er morgen kommt.

Antwort: Er sagte: „Ich komme morgen."

a. Sie sagt, dass sie ein neues Auto gekauft hat.

_____

b. Der Lehrer erklärt, dass die Prüfung leicht sein wird.

_____

c. Maria fragt, ob Peter am Wochenende Zeit hat.

_____

d. Der Direktor kündigt an, dass die Schule am Montag geschlossen bleibt.

_____

e. Der Arzt rät, dass man viel Wasser trinken soll.

_____

SCHLUSSWORT
(CONCLUSION)

As we close the final pages of this book, we reflect on the enriching journey through the German language that we have undertaken together. From revisiting the fundamental basics to exploring the rich tapestry of German culture, nature, travel, education, and leisure, your linguistic skills have not only deepened but have also become more versatile and dynamic.

Your ability to navigate complex grammatical structures, to understand and use nuanced vocabulary, and to engage with the language in a variety of contexts is a testament to your dedication and hard work. You can now confidently discuss diverse topics, from environmental issues to cultural festivities, and from travel adventures to professional scenarios, all in German.

This course was designed to build upon the foundations laid in our first book, and we hope that it has not only expanded your knowledge but also fueled your passion for the German language and culture. The journey of language learning is continuous and ever-evolving, and we encourage you to keep this momentum going.

As you move forward, here are some suggestions to further enhance your German language skills:

- **Engage in Conversations**: Seek opportunities to converse with native German speakers. This could be through language exchange meetups, online forums, or social groups.

- **Immerse in Media**: Continue to immerse yourself in German media. Watch German films, listen to German music, and read German literature to get accustomed to different dialects and colloquial language.

- **Travel**: If possible, travel to German-speaking countries. There's no better way to learn a language than by living it. Experience the culture, practice your language skills with locals, and immerse yourself in everyday German life.

- **Continuous Learning**: Consider enrolling in advanced language courses or workshops that focus on specific aspects of the language, such as business German or literary German.

- **Stay Curious**: Always keep your curiosity alive. Explore topics of personal interest in German, be it in technology, art, history, or any other field.

We bid you „*Auf Wiedersehen*" with a heart full of hope that your journey with the German language will continue to be as rewarding and fulfilling as it has been so far. May your path be filled with continuous learning, cultural exploration, and endless opportunities to use and enjoy the language.

Viel Erfolg und alles Gute auf Deinem weiteren Sprachweg!
(All the best and good luck on your continued language path!)

LÖSUNGSSCHLÜSSEL
(ANSWER KEY)

UNIT I

Ü 1.1)

A → Apfelkuchen	B → Boden	C → Chance
D → Dach	E → essen	F → Faden
G → Gitarre	H → Hase	I → Insel
J → Jacke	K → Klavier	L → Lippe
M → Maus	N → Nadel	O → Oberteil
P → Pinguin	Q → Qualle	R → Rucksack
S → Suppe	T → Tannenbaum	U → Unterhose
V → Vase	W → Windel	X → xenophob
Y → Yak	Z → Zunge	Ä → Ärger
Ö → öffnen	Ü → überprüfen	

Ü 1.2)

a. Kuchen **b.** Tasse **c.** Baum **d.** Brille **e.** Schlüssel

Ü 1.3)

Berg (mountain): der, ein

Wald (forest): der, ein

Fluss (river): der, ein

Wiese (meadow): die, eine

Stadt (city): die, eine

Sonne (sun): die, eine

Telefon (telephone): das, ein

Meer (sea): das, ein

Himmel (sky): der, ein

Stern (star): der, ein

Zug (train): der, ein

Schokolade (chocolate): die, eine

Hund (dog): der, ein

Bild (picture): das, ein

Ü 1.4)

Es war ein **sonniger/kühler/regnerischer** Tag in Blankenburg, einem **idyllischen/kleinen/beschaulichen** Dorf am Fuß eines **riesigen/bewaldeten/steilen** Berges. Am Rand des Dorfes, direkt neben dem **dichten/dunklen/ruhigen** Wald, stand ein **altmodisches/verwittertes/gemütliches** Haus mit knarzenden Dielen und **blauen/verblassten/hölzernen** Fensterläden. In diesem Haus lebte Frau Müller, eine **freundliche/runzlige/lebenslustige** alte Dame mit einem **ansteckenden/warmen/liebevollen** Lächeln und ihrem **faulen/streunenden/schläfrigen** Kater namens Gustav. Jeden Morgen, nachdem der Hahn **lautstark/fröhlich/energisch** krähte, ging sie in ihren **blühenden/wilden/gepflegten** Garten und bewunderte die **farbenfrohen/duftenden/seltenen** Blumen, die in der Morgensonne **golden/glitzernd/funkelnd** glänzten.

Heute jedoch war etwas anders. Als Frau Müller, wie gewohnt, ihren Kaffee auf der **kleinen/überdachten/windgeschützten** Veranda trank, entdeckte sie ein **großes/kleines/geheimnisvolles** Paket direkt neben ihrem Lieblingsrosenbusch. Es trug keine Adresse, nur ihren Namen in **geschwungenen/schönen/altmodischen** Lettern. Frau Müller war **überrascht/neugierig/verwundert** und entschied, es vorsichtig zu öffnen. Im Paket fand sie einen **langen/kurzen/herzlichen** Brief und ein altes **verblasstes/farbenfrohes/gerahmtes** Foto von ihr als junges Mädchen. Der Brief war von ihrer alten Schulfreundin Klara, die sie seit Jahren nicht mehr gesehen hatte. Klara schrieb, dass sie in die Stadt gezogen war und hoffte, sich bald wieder mit Frau Müller zu treffen. Das Foto war ein Andenken an ihre **glücklichen/abenteuerlichen/unbeschwerten** Jugendtage. Frau Müller war gerührt und beschloss, sofort einen Antwortbrief zu schreiben, in dem sie Klara zu einem Tee in ihrem **schattigen/sonnigen/blühenden** Garten einlud.

Ü 1.5)

Während ich dort **war**, **traf ich** meinen alten Freund Peter. Wir **unterhielten uns** lange und **erinnerten uns** an alte Zeiten. Während unserer Unterhaltung **fing es** plötzlich zu regnen an. Schnell **suchten wir** Schutz unter einem großen Baum. Als der Regen **aufhörte**, **gingen wir weiter** und **verabschiedeten uns**. Es **war** ein unerwartetes, aber schönes Treffen.

Ü 1.6)

Sie legt das Buch **auf** den Tisch und geht in die Küche. **Daraufhin** vergisst sie komplett auf das Buch. Ihr Bruder, der ins Wohnzimmer kommt, bemerkt es und nimmt es in die Hand. Er blättert es **schnell** durch und findet eine Notiz **darin**. Neugierig liest er, was auf dieser steht.
Am Abend, als die Familie beim Abendessen sitzt, spricht er Anna **darauf** an. Anna schaut überrascht, erinnert sich aber dann an das Buch und lacht. Ihr kleiner Bruder sitzt **neben ihnen** und schaut die beiden neugierig an. **Daraufhin** möchte er auch wissen, was im Buch steht. Anna verspricht **ihm,** es ihm später vorzulesen.

Nach dem Essen setzt sich die Familie **vor** den Fernseher. Doch Anna und ihr kleiner Bruder ziehen sich in ihr Zimmer zurück. **Auf** dem Sofa kuscheln sie sich zusammen und Anna beginnt, aus dem Buch vorzulesen. Es wird ein gemütlicher Abend, **weil** sie ihn gemeinsam verbringen.

Ü 1.7)

a.	Ich gebe **meiner** Freundin **das** Buch.	Hauptsatz
b.	Sie ist die Frau, **mit der** ich gestern gesprochen habe.	Relativsatz
c.	Er hat einen Hund, **der** sehr groß ist.	Relativsatz
d.	Das ist **das** Haus, in **dem** wir wohnen.	Relativsatz
e.	Sie erzählte, **dass** sie morgen kommt.	Nebensatz
f.	Der Apfel, **der vom** Tisch fällt, ist rot.	Relativsatz
g.	Das Mädchen, **dessen** Bruder krank ist, weint.	Relativsatz
h.	**Nach** dem Essen gehen wir spazieren.	Hauptsatz

UNIT 2

Ü 1.1)

Infinitiv	Präsens	Präteritum	Perfekt	Plusquamperfekt	Futur I	Futur II
spielen	ich spiele	ich spielte	ich habe gespielt	ich hatte gespielt	ich werde spielen	ich werde gespielt haben
machen	ich mache	ich machte	ich habe gemacht	ich hatte gemacht	ich werde machen	ich werde gemacht haben
gehen	ich gehe	ich ging	ich bin gegangen	ich war gegangen	ich werde gehen	ich werde gegangen sein
sehen	ich sehe	ich sah	ich habe gesehen	ich hatte gesehen	ich werde sehen	ich werde gesehen haben
schreiben	ich schreibe	ich schrieb	ich habe geschrieben	ich hatte geschrieben	ich werde schreiben	ich werde geschrieben haben
kommen	ich komme	ich kam	ich bin gekommen	ich war gekommen	ich werde kommen	ich werde gekommen sein
sprechen	ich spreche	ich sprach	ich habe gesprochen	ich hatte gesprochen	ich werde sprechen	ich werde gesprochen haben
finden	ich finde	ich fand	ich habe gefunden	ich hatte gefunden	ich werde finden	ich werde gefunden haben
bringen	ich bringe	ich brachte	ich habe gebracht	ich hatte gebracht	ich werde bringen	ich werde gebracht haben
denken	ich denke	ich dachte	ich habe gedacht	ich hatte gedacht	ich werde denken	ich werde gedacht haben

Ü 1.2)

a. „Ich habe geschrieben."
b. „Ich werde sehen."
c. „Ich machte."
d. „Ich hatte gespielt."
e. „Ich werde gefunden haben."
f. „Ich bin gekommen."
g. „Ich dachte."
h. „Ich werde bringen."
i. „Ich hatte gesprochen."
j. „Ich werde gelesen haben."

Ü 2.1)

a. Ich gehe spazieren, wenn das Wetter gut ist. — Hauptsatz und Nebensatz
b. Bringe den Müll raus! — Aufforderungssatz
c. Wann fährt der nächste Bus? — Fragesatz
d. Sie liest ein Buch, das auf dem Tisch liegt. — Hauptsatz und Nebensatz
e. Wenn du Hilfe brauchst, sage Bescheid. — Hauptsatz und Nebensatz
f. Öffne das Fenster! — Aufforderungssatz
g. Wo ist der nächste Supermarkt? — Fragesatz
h. Er spielt Fußball, um fit zu bleiben. — Hauptsatz und Nebensatz
i. Möchtest du einen Tee? — Fragesatz
j. Er schreibt einen Brief, der sehr wichtig ist. — Hauptsatz und Nebensatz

Ü 2.2)

a. Er kocht das Abendessen, **während** ich das Geschirr spüle.
b. Sie macht Yoga. **Währenddessen** bereite ich das Frühstück vor.
c. Ich schreibe E-Mails, **während** das Meeting läuft.
d. Er geht joggen, **während** sie die Nachrichten sieht.
e. Ich höre Musik, **während** ich Hausaufgaben mache.
f. Sie malt ein Bild. **Währenddessen** lese ich ein Buch.
g. Er spielt Fußball, **während** seine Freunde zuschauen.
h. Ich backe Plätzchen, **während** die Kinder spielen.
i. Sie telefoniert, **während** ihr Mann das Auto wäscht.
j. Ich putze das Haus. **Währenddessen** kauft er Lebensmittel ein.

Ü 2.3)

a. Er geht **ins** Kino. → Er geht **in das** Kino.
b. Ich warte **beim** Arzt. → Ich warte **bei dem** Arzt.
c. Wir lernen **fürs** Examen. → Wir lernen **für das** Examen.
d. Sie sitzt **im** Café. → Sie sitzt **in dem** Café.
e. Er ist **zum** Markt gegangen. → Er ist **zu dem** Markt gegangen.
f. Sie wollen **zur** Party. → Sie wollen **zu der** Party.
g. Er spielt **beim** Konzert. → Er spielt **bei dem** Konzert.
h. Wir sind **ans** Meer gefahren. → Wir sind **an das** Meer gefahren.
i. Sie wohnt **im** Altenheim. → Sie wohnt **in dem** Altenheim.
j. Ich bin **zum** Bahnhof gerannt. → Ich bin **zu dem** Bahnhof gerannt.

Ü 3.1)

Wer hat mein Buch genommen? **Es** lag hier auf **diesem** Tisch. Ich brauche **es**, um meine Hausaufgaben zu machen. **Es ist** sehr alt und enthält viele interessante Geschichten. Wenn **du es** siehst, kannst **du es** mir geben? **Ich** selbst habe überall gesucht, aber **ich** kann **es** nirgends finden. Wessen Stift ist **das**? **Er** sieht fast genauso aus wie **meiner**, aber **ich** bin sicher, **ich** habe **meinen** in **meine** Tasche getan. Kann derjenige, **der** meinen Stift hat, **ihn mir** zurückgeben? Ich brauche **ihn** für die Schule morgen. **Er** ist sehr wichtig für **mich**, weil **ich einen** Test schreiben werde.

Ü 3.2)

As this is a creative task, there is no set answer. The teacher or a study partner should check the story for correct use of relative clauses.

Ü 3.3)

a. Er liest immer, **wenn** er Zeit hat.
b. Sie war glücklicher, **als** sie jünger war.
c. **Wenn** du das Fenster öffnest, wird es frischer.
d. Ich war gerade eingeschlafen, **als** das Telefon klingelte.
e. Sie geht schwimmen, **wenn** das Wetter gut ist.
f. Er ist schneller **als** sein Bruder.
g. **Wenn** es regnet, bleiben wir zu Hause.
h. Sie sieht jünger aus, **als** sie ist.
i. **Als** er krank war, blieb er im Bett.
j. Es ist schöner, **wenn** die Sonne scheint.

Ü 3.4)

① Der Gärtner gießt die Blumen.
② Die Blumen sind schön.
} Die schönen Blumen werden vom Gärtner gegossen.

① Die Lehrerin korrigiert die Klausuren.
② Die Klausuren sind schwierig.
} Die schwierigen Klausuren werden von der Lehrerin korrigiert.

① Der Koch bereitet das Essen vor.
② Das Essen ist köstlich.
} Das köstliche Essen wird vom Koch vorbereitet.

① Der Mechaniker repariert das Auto.
② Das Auto ist alt.
} Das alte Auto wird vom Mechaniker repariert.

① Die Designerin entwirft das Kleid.
② Das Kleid ist elegant.
} Das elegante Kleid wird von der Designerin entworfen.

① Die Kinder bauen die Sandburg.
② Die Sandburg ist groß.
} Die große Sandburg wird von den Kindern gebaut.

① Der Fotograf macht die Fotos.
② Die Fotos sind scharf.
} Die scharfen Fotos werden vom Fotografen gemacht.

① Die Studenten lesen die Bücher.
② Die Bücher sind interessant.
} Die interessanten Bücher werden von den Studenten gelesen.

① Der Bauer pflanzt die Bäume.
② Die Bäume sind klein.
} Die kleinen Bäume werden vom Bauern gepflanzt.

UNIT 3

Ü 1.1)

Subjekt	Reflexives Verb	Reflexives Pronomen	Übersetzung
du	vergewisserst	**dich**	You assure (yourself)
er	vergewissert	**sich**	He assures (himself)
sie (feminin)	vergewissert	**sich**	She assures (herself)
wir	vergewissern	**uns**	We assure (ourselves)
ihr	vergewissert	**euch**	You (plural) assure (yourselves)
sie (plural)	vergewissern	**sich**	They assure (themselves)
Sie (Höflichkeitsform)	vergewissern	**sich**	You assure (yourself) (formal)

Ü 2.1)

a. Er hat vergessen, **einzukaufen**, deshalb haben wir nichts zum Abendessen.
b. Ich freue mich darauf, dich **zu sehen**.
c. Sie versucht, den Text **zu verstehen**.
d. Wir haben beschlossen, früh **aufzustehen**.
e. Es ist oft schwer, die Wahrheit **zu sagen**.
f. Die Kinder haben angefangen, **zu weinen**, weil sie müde waren.
g. Ich brauche eine Pause, um wieder zu Atem **zu kommen**.
h. Es ist gefährlich, ohne Helm **zu fahren**.
i. Wir planen, nächstes Jahr nach Deutschland **zu reisen**.
j. Sie hofft, bald einen neuen Job **zu finden**.

Ü 2.2)

a. Haus — Häus**chen**
b. Baum — Bäum**chen**
c. Tisch — Tisch**lein**/Tisch**chen**
d. Blatt — Blätt**chen**
e. Katze — Kätz**chen**
f. Vogel — Vögel**chen**
g. Stein — Stein**chen**
h. Auto — Auto**chen**/Auto**lein**

Ü 2.3)

Basiswort (Base Word)	Mit Präfix (With Prefix)	Mit Suffix (With Suffix)	Mit Präfix und Suffix (With Prefix and Suffix)
Freund	Unfreund	Freundschaft	unfreundlich
leben	beleben	lebendig	unlebendig
trinken	betrinken	trinkend	betrinkend
schreiben	beschreiben	Schreibung	Beschreibung
Spiel	Vorspiel	spielen	vorspielen
laufen	verlaufen	laufend	verlaufend
sehen	übersehen	sehend	übersehend
arbeiten	bearbeiten	arbeitend	bearbeitend

Ü 2.4)

Basiswort (Base Word)	Abgeleitete Wörter (Derived Words)
Trinken	betrinken, Trinker, Trinkwasser
Schreiben	Beschreibung, Schreibwaren, Anschreiben
Sicht	Sichtbarkeit, sichtbar, unsichtbar, Ansicht
Hören	Hörbarkeit, Gehör, Hörgerät
Bild	bilden, Abbildung, Bildung, bildlich
Lernen	Lernende, Lernmaterial, erlernen
Verstand	verstehen, Verständnis, unverständlich, Missverständnis
Schlaf	schlafen, Schlaflosigkeit, Einschlafen, Tiefschlaf
Fahren	Abfahrt, Fahrer, Fahrrad
Lesen	Leser, Lesbarkeit, Lesebuch
Bau	bauen, Bauwerk, Baustein, Bauart
Glauben	Glaube, Unglaube, Glaubwürdigkeit
Spiel	spielen, Spielplatz, Mitspieler, Vorspiel

Ü 3.1)

a. „Das ist _____ eine gute Idee!"   → mal; doch; ja
b. „Könntest du das _____ erklären?"   → mal; nicht
c. „Er spielt _____ gut Klavier."   → sehr; ziemlich
d. „Wir gehen jetzt _____ nach Hause."   → nicht
e. „Das schmeckt _____ lecker!"   → ziemlich
f. „Du bist _____ gekommen."   → doch; ja
g. „Mach das _____ auf!"   → doch
h. „Das wird _____ interessant."   → mal
i. „Sie hat _____ ja gesagt."   → doch; nicht;
j. „Kommst du _____ mit?"   → doch; nicht

Ü 3.2)

a. Sie sagt, sie werde morgen kommen.
b. Er sagt, er könne das nicht machen.
c. Wir sagen, wir seien im Kino.
d. Du sagst, du hättest Hunger.
e. Sie sagen, sie würden das Projekt beenden.
f. Ich sage, ich ginge spazieren.
g. Ihr sagt, ihr habet das Spiel gewonnen.
h. Er sagt, er werde das Auto reparieren.
i. Sie sagt, sie könne das Fenster öffnen.
j. Du sagst, du wolltest ein Eis essen.

Ü 3.3)

a. Sie behauptet, sie **habe** keine Zeit.
b. Er meint, er **könne** das nicht machen.
c. Wir denken, wir **müssten** früher aufstehen.
d. Du sagst, du **wollest** das Buch lesen.
e. Ich habe gehört, ich **solle** Sie anrufen.
f. Sie erklären, es **sei** wichtig.
g. Er glaubt, er **werde** gewinnen.
h. Wir vermuten, ihr **möget** keinen Kaffee.
i. Sie denkt, sie **könne** das lösen.
j. Ich sage, du **lägest** richtig.

Ü 3.4)

a. Du würdest früher gehen.
b. Er fände die Lösung.
c. Wir würden nach Deutschland reisen.
d. Ihr würdet im Park spielen.
e. Sie würde Abendessen kochen.
f. Es würde regnen.
g. Ich würde antworten.
h. Sie würden den Film sehen.
i. Du würdest ein Lied singen.
j. Er spräche Spanisch.

UNIT 4

Ü 1.1)

a. Er klopft **an** die Tür. anklopfen
b. Sie bindet den Schal **um**. umbinden
c. Der Junge greift **zu**. zugreifen
d. Der Mann wartet **ab**. abwarten
e. Sie hängt die Uhr **auf**. aufhängen

Ü 1.2)

| ☒ **wiedersehen** | oder | ☐ **wieder sehen** | ☒ **gutmachen** | oder | ☐ **gut machen** |

| ☒ **stattfinden** | oder | ☐ **statt finden** | ☒ **festhalten** | oder | ☐ fest halten |

| ☐ **radfahren** | oder | ☒ **Rad fahren** | ☒ **liegenbleiben** | oder | ☒ **liegen bleiben** |

(Both forms, „liegenbleiben" and „liegen bleiben", are acceptable).

| ☒ **teilnehmen** | oder | ☐ **teil nehmen** | ☒ **kennenlernen** | oder | ☒ **kennen lernen** |

(Both forms, „kennenlernen" and „kennen lernen" are acceptable according to the Duden, but „kennenlernen" is more common.)

Ü 2.1)

a. Wenn du **früh kommst**, bekommst du einen guten Platz.
b. Ich würde ihm helfen, wenn ich **könnte**.
c. Sie **wäre traurig**, wenn ihr Hund wegliefe..
d. Er würde ins Kino gehen, wenn er Geld **hätte**.
e. Wenn es morgen **regnet**, bleibt sie zu Hause.
f. Du würdest besser schlafen, wenn du weniger **fernsehen würdest.**
g. Wenn sie rechtzeitig **abfährt**, erreicht sie das Ziel pünktlich.
h. Ich würde dir das Buch leihen, wenn ich es **nicht verloren hätte**.
i. Wenn sie weiter so **hart arbeitet**, wird sie bald befördert.
j. Er **wäre froh**, wenn du ihm hilfst.

Ü 2.2)

a. **Question:** Was würdest du machen, wenn Wasser plötzlich nach Schokolade schmecken würde?

   Answer: Wenn Wasser nach Schokolade schmecken würde, würde ich den ganzen Tag nur Wasser trinken.

b. **Question:** Wie würdest du deinen Tag verbringen, wenn jede Stunde 120 Minuten hätte?

   Answer: Wenn jede Stunde 120 Minuten hätte, würde ich mehr Zeit zum Schlafen nutzen.

c. **Question:** Was würdest du tun, wenn Tiere dich um Rat fragen könnten?

   Answer: Wenn Tiere mich um Rat fragen könnten, würde ich versuchen, ihnen so gut wie möglich zu helfen.

d. **Question:** Was würdest du machen, wenn du durch Gedankenkraft Gegenstände bewegen könntest?

   Answer: Wenn ich Gegenstände mit Gedankenkraft bewegen könnte, würde ich nie wieder meine Fernbedienung suchen müssen.

e. **Question:** Wie würdest du dich verhalten, wenn jeder gelogene Satz sofort sichtbar auf deiner Stirn erscheinen würde?

   Answer: Wenn gelogene Sätze auf meiner Stirn erscheinen würden, würde ich immer die Wahrheit sagen.

The solutions provided above are merely examples. There are no fixed answers; the learner's creativity is encouraged!

Ü 3.1)

a. Es ist drei Uhr.
b. Es ist Viertel vor eins.
c. Es ist halb sieben.
d. Es ist Viertel nach neun.
e. Es ist zehn vor drei.
f. Es ist zehn nach elf.
g. Es ist fünf vor halb sechs.

Ü 3.2)

a. Bier ⟶ Das ist nicht mein **Bier**.
⟶ Das geht mich nichts an / That's none of my business.

b. Augen ⟶ Er hat Tomaten auf den **Augen**.
⟶ Er übersieht das Offensichtliche / It's as plain as the nose on your face.

c. Bauch ⟶ Sie hat Schmetterlinge im **Bauch**.
⟶ Sie ist aufgeregt oder verliebt / She has butterflies in her stomach.

d. herumreden ⟶ Um den heißen Brei **herumreden**.
⟶ Ein Thema vermeiden / To beat around the bush.

e. heißen Stein ⟶ Das ist ein Tropfen auf den **heißen Stein**.
⟶ Eine unzureichende Maßnahme / A drop in the bucket.

f. Schlips ⟶ Jemandem auf den **Schlips** treten.
⟶ Jemanden beleidigen / To step on someone's toes.

UNIT 5

Ü 1.1)

a. Er lernt viel, **damit** er die Prüfung besteht.   **Finalsatz**
b. Sie trägt einen Hut, **weil** die Sonne sehr stark ist.   **Kausalsatz**
c. Wir gehen früh schlafen, **weil** wir morgen früh aufstehen müssen.   **Kausalsatz**
d. Sie nimmt ein Medikament, **weil** sie Kopfschmerzen hat.   **Kausalsatz**
e. Er spart Geld, **damit** er sich ein neues Auto kaufen kann.   **Finalsatz**
f. Sie zieht einen Mantel an, **weil** es draußen kalt ist.   **Kausalsatz**
g. Wir machen das Fenster auf, **damit** frische Luft hereinkommt.   **Finalsatz**
h. Er isst nichts Süßes, **damit** er abnehmen kann.   **Finalsatz**
i. Sie ruft an, **weil** sie Informationen benötigt.   **Kausalsatz**
j. Er trägt Sonnencreme auf, **damit** er keinen Sonnenbrand bekommt.   **Finalsatz**

Ü 1.2)

a. Lernen → Das Lernen fällt ihr leicht.
b. Spielen → Das Spielen mit Freunden macht Spaß.
c. Reisen → Das Reisen in ferne Länder ist aufregend.
d. Singen → Ihr Singen begeisterte das Publikum.
e. Arbeiten → Das Arbeiten im Team ist effektiver.
f. Kochen → Das Kochen ist seine Leidenschaft.
g. Leben → Das Leben bietet viele Möglichkeiten.
h. Schreiben → Das Schreiben eines Romans erfordert Geduld.

Ü 1.3)

a. Das regelmäßige **Üben** ist wichtig.
b. Er hofft auf eine baldige **Gesundung.**
c. Sie vermeidet das nächtliche **Alleinelaufen.**
d. Er genießt das **Gitarrespielen.**
e. Das frühe **Aufstehen** ist schwer.
f. Sie versucht eine schnellere **Laufgeschwindigkeit.**
g. Er plant eim nächsten Jahr mit dem **Studieren** zu beginnen.

Ü 1.4)

a. „**Och nein**, ich habe den Zug verpasst!"
b. „**Wow**, was für eine Überraschung, dich hier zu sehen!"
c. „**Mmh**, das Essen schmeckt fantastisch!"
d. „**Mist**, ich habe mein Portemonnaie zu Hause vergessen!"
e. „**Oh**, das ist ja ein niedlicher Hund!"

Ü 2.1)

a. Sie versucht, **früh ins Bett zu gehen**.
b. Er hat keine Zeit, **mit seinen Freunden auszugehen**.
c. Es ist nicht leicht, **eine neue Sprache zu lernen**.
d. Wir planen, **nächsten Sommer nach Italien zu reisen**.
e. Es macht Spaß, **mit Freunden zu kochen**.
f. Sie hofft, **den Test zu bestehen**.

Ü 3.1)

Wort 1	Wort 2	Zusammengesetztes Nomen
Schlaf	Zimmer	Schlafzimmer
Kinder	Garten	Kindergarten
Buch	Regal	Bücherregal
Kaffee	Tasse	Kaffeetasse
Blumen	Vase	Blumenvase
Wasser	Flasche	Wasserflasche
Straßen	Laterne	Straßenlaterne
Auto	Bahn	Autobahn
Stadt	Plan	Stadtplan

UNIT 6

Ü 1.1)

a. **Original**: Die Kinder (Subjekt) spielen (Prädikat) im Garten (Adverbiale) Fußball (Objekt).
   Umgestellt: Im Garten spielen die Kinder Fußball.

b. **Original**: Der talentierte Musiker (Subjekt) spielt (Prädikat) eine schöne Melodie (Objekt) auf seiner Geige (Adverbiale).
   Umgestellt: Eine schöne Melodie spielt der talentierte Musiker auf seiner Geige.

c. **Original**: Sie (Subjekt) trifft (Prädikat) alte Freunde (Objekt) in Berlin (Adverbiale).
   Umgestellt: In Berlin trifft sie alte Freunde.

d. **Original**: Der alte Mann (Subjekt) liest jeden Morgen in der Bibliothek (Adverbiale) die Zeitung (Objekt).
   Umgestellt: In der Bibliothek liest der alte Mann jeden Morgen die Zeitung.

Ü 1.2)

Satz	Subjekt	Prädikat	Objekt	Adverbiale
Das Auto fährt schnell.	Das Auto	fährt		schnell
Kinder lachen im Park.	Kinder	lachen		im Park
Maria kauft im Supermarkt ein neues Buch.	Maria	kauft	ein neues Buch	im Supermarkt
Der Lehrer erklärt die Aufgabe in der Schule.	Der Lehrer	erklärt	die Aufgabe	in der Schule
Wir gehen heute ins Kino.	Wir	gehen		heute ins Kino

Ü 2.1)

a. Sie sagt: „Ich habe ein neues Auto gekauft."
b. Der Lehrer erklärt: „Die Prüfung wird leicht sein."
c. Maria fragt: „Hat Peter am Wochenende Zeit?"
d. Der Direktor kündigt an: „Die Schule bleibt am Montag geschlossen."
e. Der Arzt rät: „Man soll viel Wasser trinken."

MORE BOOKS BY LINGO MASTERY

We are not done teaching you German until you're fluent!

Here are some other titles you might find useful in your journey of mastering German:

✓ German Short Stories for Beginners

✓ Intermediate German Short Stories

✓ 2000 Most Common German Words in Context

✓ Conversational German Dialogues

But we have many more!

Check out all of our titles at www.lingomastery.com/german

www.ingramcontent.com/pod-product-compliance
Lightning Source LLC
Chambersburg PA
CBHW081445070526
44586CB00019B/2236